Cooking fish
with Ali

2012.

exquisite recipes from
around the world

By

Ali Javaheri

BARNY BOOKS

ISBN No: 1.903172.57.8

Published by: Barny Books
               Hough on the Hill
               Near Grantham
               Lincolnshire
               NG32 2BB

               Tel: 01400 250246

Type setter: Jayne Thompson

Printed by: Athenaeum Press Ltd
               Dukesway
               Team Valley
               Gateshead
               Tyne & Wear
               NE11 0PZ

               Tel: 0191 4910770

Cover photograph by: Fame Factory, Nottingham.

Illustrated fish provided by: Nick Fishmongers.
                               Victoria Centre, Nottingham

Dedication

To my sisters

Zohreh, Mansoureh,
Fattaneh and Farzaneh

whom I love very much

&

To my dad

CONTENTS

Introduction

To me cooking is only a game in which the whole family can play a role. We all had our duties in our house. Setting the table, serving the food, clearing the empty plates or simply make the tea. Even my father was called into service to buy the hot crust bread from the shop. It was a regular daily ritual.

Those early days made me discover the adventures in cooking, something that demands to be tasted and talked about, compared with other dishes, other meals or other fish varieties. An experience to be shared. Add a starter, deserts and accompany it with a good dry white wine and bingo, you have a party to remember.

In my early twenties I started to believe that careless eating could be as antisocial as careless cooking. I remember, I was in Chicago in a sort of high society restaurant when I saw a tiny tot out with his family for lunch tucking into a dish of sophisticated mussels in a cream and white wine dressing. But, why should it be surprising? I imagine this is the way subtleties should be called to our attention early on in life.

According to Nicholas Perricome, ageing is a progressive inflammatory disease that occurs at the cellular level of the body, but that it can be controlled by what you eat. So, wrinkled sagging of the skin is not the inevitable result of growing older. It is a disease, caused by bad nourishment and we have to fight it by eating healthy food and nothing is healthier than fish.

I have had the pleasure in selecting a miscellany of recipes that reflects the ways in which people from all over the world have adapted to the cooking environment in Europe, especially Britain, Asia, North America and Africa.

You will find familiar French recipes for fish in this book and when looking at the recipes of other countries, the French influence is quite noticeable. There are recipes for everyone in here. Many people may feel safer eating fish that is plain whereas others may prefer dishes that are highly flavoured. My choice of recipes has been made with a certain type of person in mind - for those people who are keen to extend their knowledge of both recognising and cooking of fish.

I sincerely hope that this book will encourage you to join me on the never ending and challenging adventure of experimenting with food from the sea.

I also hope that my cook book may tempt you to be adventurous in your food preparation. It is easier to cook imaginatively if it makes cooking more fun for you.

So, don't be frightened by your own courage. You may start with a good spirit by choosing a recipe and spread out all your ingredients on the kitchen table and then find out you don't have the fennel which is supposed to perfume the fish and then, like a wet dish cloth, doubts fall on you and dampen your good intention. Don't let that worry you. So, what is the answer? Use what you have, fresh or dried, it doesn't matter. The answer is " to experience." It may even be better than what I have suggested.

With this book, I am trying to celebrate the fish family with detailed accounts of their time in season, the kind of fish they are and the way in which they are prepared and cooked. I am also trying to guide you to greater enjoyment. This book is not to be put on the shelf and ignored. This book is for use, no matter how thumbed, greasy and crumpled it gets.

Finally, I would like to offer my thanks to those who have assisted me by reading and commenting on the composition of this book with honesty. I would sincerely like to give a world of thanks to Jayne my editor, Molly my publisher for bringing this book to fruition, and to Nick & John my local fishmongers, for their help and support. My thanks go also to you the reader, for your decision to use my books for practical information and to prepare exquisite cuisine. But above all, my special thanks from the bottom of my heart goes to Joy, the one who has made it all happen.

Enjoy!

Ali Javaheri

Foreword

In response to public demand and enthusiasts around the world, I have pleasure in presenting some of the most fascinating and exotic fish dishes in this book.

Considering the amazing variety of available sea food it is no wonder that fish has always been considered an alternative to meat dishes. However I have often wondered at the relatively small number of book publications dealing with the subject.

Although several excellent books with regards to fish have been published, it seems to me, that these have all tended to concentrate on the kind of fish and shellfish which comes to the hands of people living at or visiting the coast or the lucky ones who have a fisherman in their family.

These days you can only get your hands on a few fish from the freezer store and not much from the fresh fish cabinet of the local store. So, what happens if an ordinary man or woman in the street wants to get his hand on some fish such as pike, halibut, red snapper or John Dory? You must go to a fishmonger, fish market or the coast but I am sure you will then be able to get any fish you desire. With this in mind, I have set out to provide a universal fish cook book with recipes as much for the person living at the coast as for those who live inland. I have also become increasingly aware over the years of just how little fundamental understanding there is about cooking fish. I have therefore provided a broad ranging source of information on the entire subject. Every fish, be it little frozen Icelandic prawns or Crayfish tails, they all find their place in this book. As for the recipes, I must admit to a personal special fondness for salmon and king prawns.

So, browse through my book a few pages at a time, select the recipes, test the dishes, invite your close friends or family and if they are happy, then throw a party. You will find this repertoire of recipes more than ample to create menus for your friends and soon you will be able to call yourself a super cook.

Happy cooking

Author's note

Looking back over my thirty odd years as a chef and restaurateur I have noticed the change in attitude of people with regards to eating fish with the exception of fish and chips which is cod or haddock, or trout and salmon. Yet, although we are surrounded by water, we have little knowledge about sea food and fish in particular.

When I look at other cookery books I feel that the language used by chefs is often technical and the wording difficult to understand. If I was explaining to you my friend over a cup of cappuccino how to make these same dishes this would not be the language I would use. In this book I have tried to keep to the English language we use in everyday life. I may be criticised by some experts for this, but that would not change the fact that I am writing this book for you the reader and not the expert chefs or the writers.

Every effort has been made for the original recipes to be intact. Modern contemporary dishes are all tested and holding good. Most of the dishes are individual portions, with the exception of snacks, accompaniments, soups and some of the starters which are clearly stated as batch recipes.

Although I have given measurements in both metric and imperial weights, please use these as guide lines as the individual taste differs from person to person and I don't wish you to think of cooking as some sort of mathematical equation.

Wine is always white and dry unless otherwise stated. Flour is always plain, sugar is always white and pepper is always black unless otherwise stated. Butter and olive oil are used in most cases. Oven temperatures are set at 180 degrees Celsius, 350 degrees Fahrenheit, or gas mark 4 as standard.

I have tried to use ingredients that are accessible to everyone without having to search the most expensive markets to make a dish. Please experiment and give yourself a free hand and I am sure you will find cooking fun and easy.

Ali

How do they do that?

The questions most people ask are "how do they do this or that?" In this chapter I have tried to answer most, if not all your questions.

Filleting - to fillet a fish, you have to cut down either side of the bone, work down towards the outside and keep as close to the bone as possible. Flat fish don't need gutting but round fish like salmon and trout etc. need to be gutted by cutting open the belly and then washing the cavity under running cold water. Cut off the head and tail and finally cut right down both sides of the back bone and there you go, you have two fillets with skins on.

To skin the fillet - dip the fingers of one hand into salt in order to be able to grip the tail of the fillet. Using the other hand, hold the knife and slide down against the skin. If you are cooking a whole fish, make sure that you first remove the scales by scraping the fish with the back of your knife under cold running water.

Freezing - fish can be kept (3-6 months) in the freezer and even longer - up to (9-12 months) providing you gut the fish and freeze it unwrapped, then take it out and dip it in cold water to increase the glaze before wrapping and re-freezing.

Smoking – Traditionally smoking takes place in a smoking house but, less traditionally in a smoke machine. Smoking is normally done over oak sawdust and sometimes with black peppercorn or with a mixture of salt, olive oil, Demerara sugar and dark rum. Examples of hot smoked fish are trout and mackerel, and examples of cold smoked fish are haddock, whiting and herring (kippers).

Salting – the salting process takes place in a wooden barrel over 2-3 days. It is then unsealed and generous amounts of brine are poured over the fish. The barrel is then resealed and turned from time to time for seven days, after which the fish is ready to be eaten. If they are to be smoked, the fish is normally soaked in cold fresh water overnight and then hung at the top of the smoke house.

Dried – for drying, first clean and wash the fish in salted water and then hang it outside, with a cover over. Dried fish does not need to be refrigerated and it will keep for up to a period of two years.

Lets talk about fish!

Fish is wonderful, inviting and irresistible for its healthy diet, being low in saturated fat and carbohydrates as well as being rich in vitamins A and D. Fish also contains protein and minerals and can easily be digested. Every time I talk about fish I bubble over with great enthusiasm as if I am cooking it or eating it.

Choosing fish – Choose fish that are as fresh as possible. The eyes should be bright and clear. The gills should be scarlet and the body as firm as possible. When you press on the skin with your finger tips and make a dent it should not rapidly disappear. Fillets should have a glossy gleam to the flesh.

Buying fish – Generally, most flat and round fish have as much skin and bone as useable fillets. Only half of the weight of the fish you buy is eatable.

In my restaurants and the ones where I have had the privilege to work in, we always worked on the following portion sizes: 3-4 oz (90-125g) for a first course and 7-8 oz (215-250g) for the main course. When serving the whole fish one can get away with less. The only exception to the rule is fish tails such as monkfish tail, John Dory, gurnard and similar large headed fish and all shellfish in general.

Cleaning fish - For cleaning shellfish such as mussels and clams, leave the scrubbed live mussels in a sink of salty water and sprinkle half a cup of oatmeal over them. After a few hours, you will notice that all the sand and mud inside the bodies has been ingested by the oatmeal.

Fish talk

I assume that you are familiar with the basic grammar of cooking and have a liberal repertoire of spices and herbs, oils and vinegars, condiments and vegetables. Before taking you around the world and showing you all the oriental, Indian, South African and Chinese ways and the way in which east meets west with regards to the cooking of fish and providing you with a range of starters and main course recipes which promises to be both a diversity of taste and a selection of easy to make elaborate fish dishes, I want to first start by dividing fish into three section as follows:

Shellfish – Clams, crabs, crayfish, lobster, mussels, prawns, oysters and shrimps are only a few varieties of the Shellfish family.

Fresh water fish – Salmon, trout, perch, pike, roach, trench, carp, eels, grayling and bream are examples of fresh water fish.

Sea fish – Can be divided as follows:
1. **Deep sea water fish** are also known as white or demersal fish and include anchovies, sea bass, sea bream, brill, escalor, haddock, halibut, john dory, monk fish, mullet (red/grey), octopus, plaice, sardine, skate, smelt, sole (lemon/dover), squid, sturgeon, tuna and turbot.
2. **Surface sea water** also known as pelagic or oily fish and these include kippers, sprats, bloaters, pilchards, herrings and whitebait.

****

There are interesting sauces and garnishes for the most common and classical fish dishes. Refer to pages 39 - 54.

There are also interesting and appropriate modern contemporary fish dishes with mouth watering sophisticated sauces and recipes which are dealt with on pages 91 - 139.

Fish varieties

Not all fish are cooked in the same way. Although we can obtain most fish all year round, be it fresh or frozen, it is good to know when they are freshly available or in season. Always, ask your fishmonger.

Cod's family:
1. **Haddock** is sold as fillet. It is good for deep frying and as steak for shallow frying. Haddock fillets weigh 6 oz / 185g per portion. Haddock can also be smoked and should always be cooked before being eaten.
2. **Hake** is usually sold as steak or fillets. It is good for frying and should be skinned before cooking. Approximate weight per portion is 6 oz / 185g.
3. **Coley** is good for fish pies or soups. Approximate weight per portion is 6 oz / 185g.
4. **Whiting** has a gelatinous texture and is used mostly for making pâté, fish balls and terrines.
5. **Cod** is sold as fillets and can be smoked. Cod is good for frying and should be skinned before cooking. Smoked cod's roe is used for pâté or taramasalata.

Trout's family:
1. **Rainbow trout's** natural habitat is lakes but these days it tends to be commercially fish farmed. Trout is good for baking in the oven or grilling and weighs around 10 oz / 310g.
2. **Sea trout** is also known as salmon trout because of its pink flesh and is good for grilling and baking.
3. **Salmon** should not be over cooked. Only a few fish can match its flavour. It can be purchased whole, as steaks or fillets and it can be poached, grilled, baked or shallow fried. Allow 6-7 oz / 185-215g per portion.
4. **Bass** is also known as sea bass or 'loup de mer' meaning sea wolf in French. It is a big, beautiful fish and there is some argument that it is from the trout family although it greatly resembles salmon. Allow 12-14 oz / 375-435g of whole fish per person.

Haddock and smoked haddock

Salmon steak and fillet

Sole

Plaice

Sea bream is also known as porgy on the east coast of America and is often mistaken for snapper which it resembles in looks but not in taste. It weights between 1 - 3 lbs or ½ - 1½ kilograms.

Sole People are confused when it comes to sole. Everyone in Britain thinks that there is a sole called lemon sole. In fact, there is only one sole and that comes from Dover. Allow 8 - 10 oz / 250 - 310g filleted per person, or 12 - 14 oz / 375 - 435g for two people.

Plaice in some restaurants is used as a substitute for sole or lemon sole and this deceit often goes unnoticed by the customer because the taste and texture of the fish is not dissimilar although the cost is much cheaper.

Snapper the best red snappers come from the Caribbean or east coast of America. The Mediterranean variety comes frozen and is almost as cheap and as good. Allow 9 - 10 oz / 280 - 310g per person.

Grey mullet is a long silver grey fish which needs de-scaling before cooking. It is perfect for stuffing and weighs around 1-1¼ lbs/500-625g and should serve 2 persons.

Red mullet is a totally different fish to grey mullet as it comes from a different family and has a different taste and texture. It needs to be scaled, gutted and sealed before cooking. If small, allow two 7oz / 215g fish per person.

Monk fish is also known as Angler fish and the tail is the only part that can be eaten. It is perfect for kebabs, grilling or pan frying. Allow 5-6 oz / 155 - 185g per person.

Halibut can be several metres long and is a very expensive fish to buy. It is sold as steaks and these can be skinned either before or after cooking. Smoked halibut is very popular in Denmark. Allow 6 oz / 185g per person.

Skate comes from the shark family and the wing is the only part which is eaten. The flesh is both firm and filling. Allow 8 oz / 250g per person.

Turbot flesh is not as dry or meaty as halibut but restaurants charge the earth for it. Turbot can be poached or grilled and in the form of steaks allow 8oz / 250g per person. Turbot should be skinned before being pan fried or oven baked.

Brill looks like turbot but its flesh is not as white or as firm and it weighs between 1 - 5 lb / 500 - 2.25kgs. Brill should be skinned before cooking and 6 oz / 185g allowed per person.

Monkfish tail

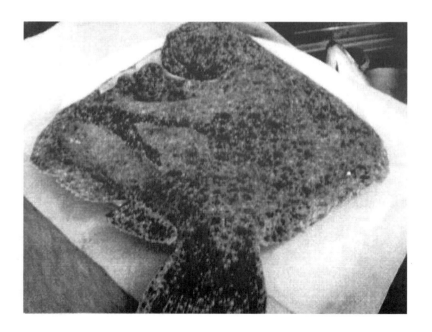

Turbot

Tuna is imported from the Mediterranean and it is good for grilling, casseroles, salads and sandwiches. Allow 6 - 8 oz / 185 - 250g per person.

Sword fish is expensive, meaty and full of flavour. It comes in the form of steaks and can be grilled or pan fried. The skin may be removed before or after cooking. It is very popular served with Cajun spices and salad. Allow 8oz / 250g per person.

Oily fish such as herrings, sardines and sprats are easy to grill and may be served with sharp sauces.

Swordfish   Tuna   Halibut

Sardines (at the back) **Whitebait**

Cleaning and preparing shellfish

Mussels

The best mussels are the ones from the open sea as they are less likely to be polluted. Most of the ones we buy are from the fishmonger and are safe to eat. Purchased mussels are normally cleaned and ready to be used. When buying mussels or any shellfish which has lots of mud and sand inside, the procedure would be the same.
First use a thick bladed knife to remove the seaweeds, beards and barnacles, then place the scrubbed live mussels into a sink of salted water and sprinkle half a cup of oatmeal over them. After a few hours you will notice that all the sand and the mud from inside the bodies has been ingested by the oatmeal.

Lobster

When buying lobster, try to get the live ones rather than the ready cooked ones from your fishmonger. The problem with the ready cooked ones is that you don't know how they have been cooked. Whether in salted water or vinegar or just water and how long ago they were cooked.
Having decided that you are going to get a live lobster and cook it yourself the following are tips you should know. When you move the lobster, the tail should spring back. To cook the lobster all you need to do is place it in a large pan of salted boiling water for half an hour. Finally to eat lobster you have to crack the shell open and pick out the flesh, which is messy but worth it.

Oysters

If you are right handed then follow the procedure below and if you are left handed just reverse the handling preparation.

1. Most oysters that are bought from a fishmonger are already cleaned. If however you need to clean your oysters follow the exact recipe as for mussels on the previous page.
2. To get inside the oyster, hold the oyster in your left hand and the knife in the right hand.
3. Insert the tip of the knife into the hinge of the oyster shell and worry away at it until it opens.
4. Slide the blade into the centre against the top shell and cut the muscle that joins the oyster to its shell as close to the flat top shell as possible.
5. Lift off the top shell, keeping the bottom shell upright.
6. Pick out any pieces that are broken.
7. Drizzle some lemon juice over the oyster and slide into your mouth without cooking.

Squids

Squid is also known as octopus and is served in restaurants as starters when ringed and deep fried, or as a main course if stuffed. To clean the squid you have to:-

1. Reach into the body with your fingers and pull out the insides which are attached to the head.
2. Pull the purple coloured skin off the body.
3. Remove the two fins.
4. Cut off the tentacles from the head and inside.
5. Remove the ink sac from the rest of the insides. This is easily identifiable and is used for making ink sauce.
6. Wash the body and the squid is ready to be ringed or stuffed.

Cleaning and filleting
flat and round fish

Like most people, I am not an enthusiast of frozen fish or frozen anything for that matter, not even ice cream. But the world we live in is not so perfect and we sometimes have leftovers because we have either cooked more than enough food or we have bought too much and have to freeze some to prevent it from going bad.

One important thing you have to remember is that if you intend to skin fish, you don't have to de-scale it or cut off the fins, but you will need to remove the guts if this has not already been done.

Round fish

Almost all round fish are treated in the same way - de-scaled, gutted and fins removed as follows:-

1. Snip off the fins with kitchen scissors.
2. Working from the tail to head, use the back of the knife to remove any scales.
3. Remove the intestine by slitting the fish along its belly from the head to the anal fin.
4. Give the cavity a good wash, and then dry with kitchen paper.

Flat fish

Almost all flat fish are treated in the same way. No gutting is required as this is done at sea. No de-scaling is required for most flat fish. All you have to do is to snip off the side fins with kitchen scissors and trim the tail fin.

Filleting round and flat fish

Round fish e.g. "salmon":

1. Scale, gut and fin the fish before filleting as follows:-

2. Lay the fish on its side on a chopping board with its back towards you. If you are right handed the head should be on your right.

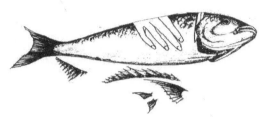

3. Hold the fish steady with your left hand and with the knife in your right hand slice along the back bone from head to tail, cutting just deep enough to expose the entire back bone.

4. Make a cut from behind the gills across the neck of the fish to separate the top fillet from the head.

5. Hold the head end of the fillet and insert the knife against the skeleton, then cut down the length of the fillet with short sharp strokes to detach it from the bones.

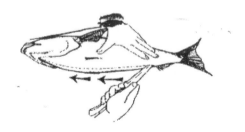

6. Hold the fish by the top of the exposed back bone, then press the flat of the knife in order to separate the fillet from the bone.

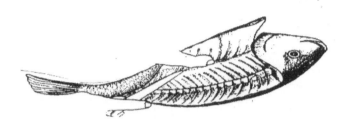

7. Lay the fillet skin side down on a chopping board.

8. Hold the tail end with your fingers, dipped in salt, to prevent it from slipping.

9. Cut free a little of the flesh from the skin and lift it up with your left hand fingers (if right handed) and then hold the skin down flat against the chopping board.

10. Insert the knife at a slight angle between the flesh and the skin and applying gentle pressure use forward short sharp strokes, to separate the fillet from the skin.

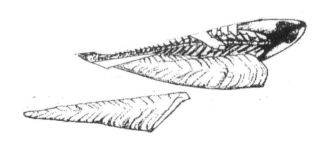

Flat fish e.g. "sole":

In general most restaurants, when cooking flat fish, attempt to remove the dark skin and leave the white skin on to hold the fish together.

1. Gut and clean the fish before filleting as follows:-
2. Place the fish on the chopping board with the dark skin uppermost and the tail towards you.
3. Make an incision through the skin across the point at which the tail joins the body.

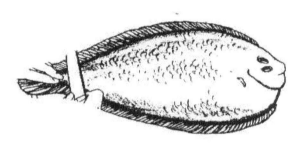

4. Slip your thumb under the skin and grip the tail firmly. (Dip your fingers in salt for a good grip.)
5. Hold the tail firmly down on the board with your left hand and grasping the loose end of the skin with the right hand, rip it towards the head of the fish and then pull it right off.

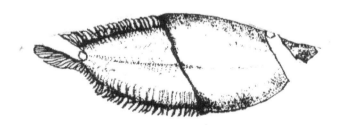

6. Now turn the fish over and making a slit through the white skin at the tail end, pull the skin off in the same way.

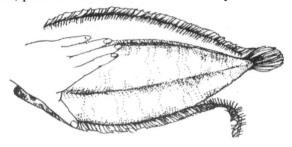

7. Lay the skinned fish on the board with its head towards you.
8. Hold the fish head with your left hand. Hold the side bones from the tail with your right hand and pull firmly towards the head.
9. Turn the fish over and repeat, before cutting off the tail bones.
10. Now place the fish on the board again with its head towards you.
11. From the head to tail, using a sharp knife, cut lengthways through to the backbone.

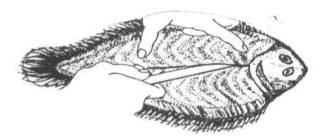

12. Starting from the head, insert the knife at an angle between the flesh and the rib bones and with short strokes, keeping the blade close to the bones, prise off the fillet.

13. Cut away the right hand fillet in the same way.

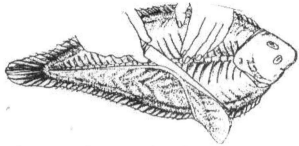

14. Turn the sole over and remove the other two fillets again using the same method.

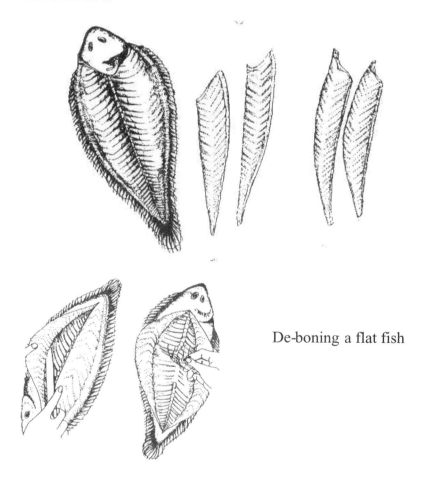

De-boning a flat fish

The principles of cooking fish

There are several ways in which fish is cooked but the most important principal is never to over cook it. Try to keep the temperature between 140°-160° C. You can cook fish by:

1. Poaching
2. Steaming
3. Baking
4. Frying
5. Grilling
6. Bread crumbing
7. Battering
8. Deep frying
9. Shallow frying
10. Braai-ing
11. Marinating
12. Preserving

Poaching
To poach means to simmer in a frying pan in a little liquid. No butter or oil is used. Almost all fish are good for poaching except hake which will break up.

Steaming
To steam means to cook the fish without immersing it in any liquid. In most cases fish kettles are used for steaming but you can place the fish between two plates over a saucepan with boiling water. It takes longer to cook but none of the juices are lost. Today beautiful bamboo steamers from the east are available from some superstores.

Baking
One of my favourite ways of cooking fish is to bake it in the oven with sauce or a liquid of some sort, like roast meat, but without having to cover it with aluminium foil. The temperature must be 180° C / 350° F if it is baked with liquid.

Frying
Fried fish still holds pride of place when served with chips amongst South African families and with parsley and coriander rice among Iranian families. Frying is the quickest way to cook fish.

Grilling

The main principal when grilling is to pre-heat the grill to ensure even heat penetration. Before grilling fish make deep slanting cuts in the fish for the heat to penetrate. Baste using a mixture of clarified butter mixed with oil. Turn the fish during grilling by using two spoons, one under the front and one under the tail, to avoid breaking. Always season with salt and pepper after grilling to ensure the fish does not form a crisp outer crust.

Bread crumbing

Breadcrumbs are made of bread but for a crunchier coating try using oatmeal or sesame seeds. These days you can make your own breadcrumbs by using a blender or food processor to finely chop up old white bread. It is necessary to first dredge the fish in flour and then beaten egg. After bread crumbing, the fish should be placed in the fridge or somewhere cold to 'bread and set' for 15 minutes.

Battering

Batter is used to protect the flesh of fish from hot oil. Batters come in different textures. Fish batter should be the consistency of thick cream. Don't beat the batter too much and make sure it is lump free. Cover and leave for at least half an hour before using. Do not waste any unwanted batter - this can be used to dip vegetables in before frying them or to make battered onion rings. To form the crispiest of crisp batters for one kilogram of fish:- Sift together 240g of self raising (cake) flour and a pinch of salt in a bowl and mix together with 2 tablespoons of oil. Make a well in the centre. Gradually stir in the water, mixing well to ensure that the mixture does not become lumpy and then beat until it forms a batter. Allow to stand for an hour before whisking in the whites of two eggs before use.

Deep frying

Pre heat the oil to 190°C / 375° F. Make sure that the fish is coated with breadcrumbs or is battered. Let your eye be your guide as to how long it takes for a fish to cook. As for temperature, use a fat thermometer. Always lift the fish from the fat using a slotted spoon.

Shallow frying

When it comes to shallow frying, you should use a thick heavy frying pan. Fill the frying pan half full or half way up the fish with oil. Make sure the oil or mixed butter and oil is hot but not hot enough to burn the fish. (If using butter make sure it is clarified butter.) Turn the fish only once during the frying and allow 4-5 minutes for each side. In the case of sole fillet allow 2-3 minutes on either side. Thick fillets may need 4 or 5 minutes.

Braai-ing

When you grill outdoors, you are grilling above heat and not below and this is called braai-ing. The secret of good braai-ing is to make a good bed of hot coals. This is something of an art form, with men in particular as its prime exponents. A hand full of dried herbs and twigs from fragrant plants such as fennel, rosemary and bay added to the coals, enhances the fish.

Marinating

Every chef I have worked with tend to use their own selection of marinades for the preparation of fish. The outcome each time is different but fantastic. But, what is a marinade?

A marinade is a seasoned liquid in which the fish is steeped and left for a period of time in order for the ingredients (seasoning) to impregnate the flesh, flavouring it as well as tenderising it. The marinade mixture is very simple and consists of some oil, some wine and some lemon juice. The oil is to prevent moisture loss and the lemon because of its acidity to soften the fish fibres. You can add crushed garlic, chopped onion, any herbs such as marjoram, chopped parsley or tarragon, soya sauce, Tabasco or even sherry.

Preserving

Before the advent of freezers, if fish was not stored carefully it would have spoiled quickly. So, what did they use or do to prevent it from spoiling?

Fish was either salted or pickled or smoked hot or cold. Hot smoking, is when a salted fish is smoked at a temperature high enough to cook the fish, examples being smoked mackerel and angel fish. Cold smoking, is when a salted fish is smoked at a lower temperature and then cooked before being eaten. Examples of cold smoked fish are kippers and haddock.

Shellfish talk

What we know about shellfish is that the flesh is surrounded by soft or hard shells but what most of us don't know is how to clean them, cook them or even eat them. This may be the reason why there is so little interest in the consumption of shellfish. In spite of the many varieties of shellfish available there are some people who haven't even tried it once. With this in mind, I will try and simplify the steps of how to recognize and deal with different varieties of shellfish.

Mussels

Mussels are cheap to buy and live in hard black shells. Mussels in the British Isles come from areas such as Devon and East Anglia and must be cleaned and washed with oatmeal (See page 18). Imported frozen mussels come from France and Holland and are usually cleaned and prepacked. Things that must be remembered about mussels is to discard all with broken shells as well as those which float or when you can hear water inside when shaken. To cook, place the mussels in a large saucepan with a little water, wine and herbs and cook for 5 minutes, shaking the pan occasionally. Discard any that have not opened.

Cockles

Cockles are mainly sold de-shelled. Once cockles are cleaned and washed, they are ready to be eaten with some sort of sauce such as vinegar or the juice of fresh lemons. Cockles are also used in seafood salads or cooked in pasta sauces or risotto.

Clams

These hard shelled fish, with a width of almost 3 inches (8cm), are sold live like mussels and can be steamed opened. Clams can also be bought preserved in jars with some sort of oil or vinegar. Italians call clams " Vongole " and they use them in salads, in sauces for pasta dishes and risottos.

Oysters

Oysters are one of the most expensive shellfish there are. Although now eaten mainly by the rich, they were in earlier times eaten by the poor. Oysters come graded from 1 - 4 according to their size, 1 being the largest. Oysters can be eaten cooked although some people prefer them raw. Whatever the preference, they should be eaten fresh and should be opened at the very last moment with a strong knife and by applying a sharp jerk between the two shells. After opening the shell, remove the oyster and place it on one half of the shell to serve.

Prawns

Prawns have grey shells and are about 2½ inches or 6cm long uncooked. Prawns may also be bought cooked, peeled and headed, fresh or frozen. When buying frozen prawns always consider 35% of the weight as ice. Prawns from India are cheap and good for using in curries. Prawns from Norway or Scotland are of a higher quality and more expensive. Mediterranean prawns are very expensive and are 4-5 inches or 10-13 cm in length with segmented bodies. The body shells of these prawns can be removed but they are usually cooked with the head on and this acts as a utensil for the fingers to hold the prawn with when dipping in sauces at the table. In restaurants shellfish are usually served accompanied by finger bowls for washing as most people eat them with their fingers. To peel prawns, simply hold by the middle and pull off the head and tail, then pull the leg downwards. The shell will detach enabling you to pick and eat the flesh quite easily.

Scampi

Also known as Norwegian prawns or Dublin Bay prawns, scampi has pale pink shells which go orange in colour when cooked. Frozen scampi is sold in Chinese and Far-Eastern supermarkets. The term Scampi is used when the tail is breaded.

Shrimps

Shrimps are very small crustaceans with brownish shells measuring 1-1½ inches or 2.5 - 4 cm in length. Shrimps are fiddly to peel and can be eaten with the thin shell on but if peeled, they make a good sauce. If in America or Canada, don't be so surprised to hear all types of prawns referred to as shrimps, as rightly, they all are from the shrimp family.

Scallops

Scallops are ribbed bivalves, with edible parts which are served opened in half rounded shells, ready to be eaten. Should you ever need to open them yourself, follow the same instruction as for oysters.

Throw away the thin wavy part round the edge and with a sharp knife cut horizontally into two. If you are using the rounded shell wash and scrub this with a nailbrush. Smaller versions of scallops are known as queens and are widely available.

Crabs

Crabs have large smooth shells and weigh between 1 – 4 lbs or 500g – 2kg, the average weight being almost 2 lbs or 1 kilogram. When buying crab consider only 35% of the weight as meat. Before purchasing fresh crab shake them slightly to make sure that there is no water sloshing around inside. When buying ready cooked crab make sure the claws are still attached. Male crabs are called cocks and these have bigger claws and aprons (the triangular flap on the underside) than hens or female crabs. Frozen crabmeat comes in 1 lb or 500g bags and crabsticks are made from Alaskan Coley in Japan.

One widely available variety of English crab known as the **spider crab** is exported to France as a delicacy. It has smaller claws and thinner legs, resembling that of a spider. To cook crabs throw them into a pan of boiling water and put the lid on. Allow 15 minutes per 1 lb or 500g and cool them in the liquid.

Lobsters

Most lobsters weight about 1½ lbs or 750g and are enough for two people. Lobsters sold in markets are usually cooked. Live lobsters are dark blue in colour and turn to a bright orange red when cooked. The male lobster is smaller than the female but has bigger claws. It also has a narrower tail with flatter sides.

Crawfish tail

Crawfish tail is a kind of rock lobster and is called **homard** in French and not langoustine which is in fact crawfish. Frozen crawfish tail is widely available. It is brownish in colour and has smaller claws than lobster.

Crayfish tail

These small fresh water shellfish are very popular in France and are known as **"Écrevisse."** Crayfish tails are smaller than Dublin bay prawns and have a very green – grey, to blackish colour when raw.

Prawns   **Crab**   **Oysters**

Crayfish

Frogs legs   **Snails**

American Scallops   Cray Fish   English Scallops

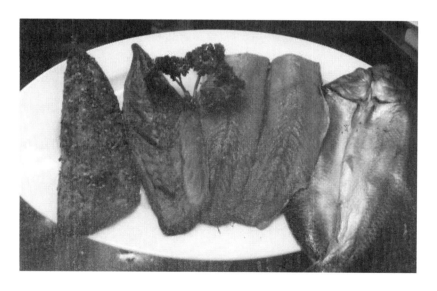

Smoked Mackrel

Preparation For Making sauces from Classic to Modern Recipes

Stocks

Stock is absolutely vital to make or produce any good dishes but when it comes to fish it becomes as important as air to me. Of course, this is because I find the flesh gets enhanced with lots of flavour and I feel that justice has been done.

Fish stock

Every single chef that I have worked with has had their own special way of making sauces and although, I must confess, they were all very delicious, when it came to making fish stock they all had one thing in common. The classic recipes were used and these don't even take more than a minute to put together and less than 10 minutes to cook. Just follow these simple steps:

1. Place in a saucepan some chopped root vegetables such as onion, celery, leek, fennel, celeriac etc.
2. Use all the trimmings, shells, bones and skin from the fish and place in the same pan.
3. Cover with water, almost an inch over the ingredients, bring to the boil and let it simmer for 10 minutes.
4. Drain the stock into a bowl and let it cool. Discard the vegetables and trimmings.

You may add your wine and herbs such as parsley, tarragon, etc. either when you add the water or when you make your sauces.

Shellfish reduction

This is a perfect stock to make terrine and mousse with because of its full flavour, essence and colour. This stock is also simple and doesn't take long to make.

1. Place only the shells from the prawns and some whole prawns in a saucepan.
2. Add a knob of butter, some chopped tarragon and a pinch of Cayenne pepper.
3. Add some roughly chopped onion, celery, carrots and 2-3 tomatoes to the pan.
4. Fill the pan with fish stock, bring to the boil, simmer for 10 minutes and cool.

Court bouillon

This is also fish stock and, because of its strong flavour and essence, it is used for flavouring fish soup, poaching in general, and especially for salmon and skate. It can also be used for making sauces.

1. In a large saucepan, place one onion, two carrots and two celery sticks (roughly chopped).
2. Add one pint water, a glass of white wine vinegar and two glasses of dry cider.
3. Bring to the boil over a high heat with 2 bay leaves, a pinch of whole black peppercorn and little salt.
4. Lower the heat and simmer for 30 minutes. Strain the liquid and let it cool to infuse before use.

Classical fish sauces & dressings

In this chapter, I have only given you the classical recipes which are both widely known and used and are simple to make.

Velouté

In the old days, flour and butter were used to thicken a sauce but in modern cookery, there is a lighter approach. Sauces are thickened with lots of butter and cream and air rather than roux.

1. Place a pint of fish stock in a large pan and bring to the boil over a high heat.
2. In a separate saucepan melt 2oz / 50g butter and add 2oz / 50g flour and stir constantly with a whisk over a low heat.
3. Gradually, add the hot stock as you stir until the texture of the mixture is smooth in appearance and then simmer for 30 minutes.
4. Pass the sauce through a conical strainer into a bowl and leave it to cool to infuse before use.

Beurre blanc

To make this sauce which is not at all complicated you will need, 60g / 2oz of chopped shallots, 6 tablespoons water, 2 tablespoons white wine vinegar, 2 tablespoons double cream, 4 tablespoons dry white wine and 7oz / 215g of unsalted butter.

1. Put the shallots, water, white wine and vinegar into a small pan, bring to the boil and let all the juice evaporate.
2. Add the cream and let it reduce a little, remove from the heat and whisk in the butter a little at a time, until it has all been amalgamated.

Beurre rouge

To make this sauce, all you need is 2oz / 60g chopped shallots, 7oz / 200g unsalted butter, 2 glasses of red wine and a pinch of sugar.

1. Put the shallots, sugar and red wine in a saucepan over a medium heat and cook until only a little sauce is left.
2. Take off the heat and whisk in the butter a little at a time, until it has all been amalgamated.

Hollandaise

This is a hot butter sauce and very rich but, by increasing the water and the egg yolks, an altogether lighter and more agreeable sauce is made. Hollandaise sauce is a very easy sauce to make especially if you own a liquidiser.

To make this sauce, all you need is four egg yolks, 4oz / 125g unsalted butter, four tablespoons of water, freshly squeezed lemon juice and a little salt and cayenne pepper.

1. Place the butter in a saucepan to clarify.
2. Place a stainless steel bowl over a larger saucepan half filled with water (being simmered on a low heat).
3. Pour the 4 tablespoons of water into the bowl, add the egg yolks and whisk the mixture until a creamy sabayon is reached.
4. Remove the pan from the heat, whisk in the butter a ladleful at a time, season with lemon juice, salt and cayenne pepper.

Hot related fish sauces

Now that we know how easy it is to make a good fish stock, we can enhance the flavour of our fish sauces by adding the fish stock to the liquid, then simmer the sauce to reduce before serving. The following recipes are the ones you are most likely to see at the dinner tables in restaurants:

Allemande, Americaine, Bearnaise, Bechamel, Bread, Italienne, Soubisse, Normande, Mornay, Lyonnaise, Genevoise and Tomate.

Allemande sauce

This sauce is also known as **parisienne,** a name which is more logical and proper and has been adopted by several chefs. This recipe is for the preparation of one litre of Allemande sauce.

What you need
1 litre / 1¾ pints Velouté – see recipe page 39
540 ml / 18 fl oz white stock
220 ml / 7 fl oz mushroom cooking liquor
5 egg yolks
100 g / 3 ½ oz butter
Juice of one fresh lemon
Pinch of grated nutmeg
Pinch of coarsely ground pepper

How to make it:
In a heavy shallow pan, place the stock, mushroom liquor, egg yolks, lemon juice, pepper and nutmeg, mix well together with a whisk and then add the Veloute. Bring to boil and simmer to reduce by one third. Pass through a fine strainer or tammy cloth. Now, coat the surface of the sauce with a little of the butter to prevent a skin forming, then add the rest of the butter before using.

Sauce tomate

This is not the same as the tomato sauce prepared and served with our meat and vegetable dishes. The recipe below is to make 5 litres or 9 pints of sauce.

What you need:
100g / 3 ½ oz butter
150g / 5 oz flour
150g / 5 oz onion, roughly diced
150g / 5 oz carrots, roughly diced
6 kg / 13 lb fresh tomatoes
2 litre / 3 ½ pint stock
2 cloves of garlic
2 Bay leaves
Pinch of salt and pepper and a sprig of thyme

How to make it:
1. Melt the butter in a big heavy pan. Add vegetables, bay leaves, and thyme and fry.
2. Sprinkle in the flour, stir and pour in the chopped fresh tomatoes and stock, and bring to boil.
3. Add garlic and seasoning and stir. Cover with a lid and simmer for 2 hours.
4. Pass through a fine strainer into a clean pan, stir and re-boil for a further 5 minutes.
5. Pour into a basin and coat the surface with butter to prevent the formation of skin.

Sauce Italienne

Italienne sauce is basically used for the preparation of many small entrees or starters. When this sauce is used for a fish dish, fish stock should be reduced and added to the sauce.

Place 125g (4 oz) lean cooked ham, finely diced in a large saucepan, with 1½ pints of demi glace and 60 ml / 4 tablespoons of dry vermouth. Bring to the boil and simmer for 5-6 minutes. Just before serving add a tablespoon of mixed tarragon, parsley and chervil.

Sauce Bearnaise

What you need:
500g / 1 lb butter
220ml / 7 fl oz of white wine vinegar
30g / 1 oz tarragon leaves, finely chopped
4 tablespoons shallots, finely chopped
Sprig of chopped chervil
6 egg yolks
Pinch of salt and crushed peppercorn
Pinch of cayenne pepper

How to make it:
1. Place the white wine vinegar in a small pan with shallots, tarragon, chervil, salt and peppercorn, bring to boil and simmer to reduce by two thirds and allow to cool.
2. Add the egg yolks to the reduction over a gentle heat and whisk adding the butter a little at a time.
3. When the butter has been completely incorporated, pass through a fine strainer, correct the seasoning and add a pinch of cayenne pepper.
4. Finish by mixing in a little tarragon and chervil.

Béchamel sauce

As I described in my previous book "Elaborate Cooking Uncovered", Béchamel is another name for white sauce. I also explained that there are a variety of different methods used to make béchamel sauce. Here I explain another method. The quantities used make 5 litres (9 pints) of sauce.

What you need:
650g /1lb 5oz white Roux –using 300g /10 oz butter and
          350g / 12½ oz plain flour
5 litres / 9 pints boiling milk
300g / 10 oz lean veal
2 finely sliced small onions
1 sprig of thyme
50g / 2 oz butter
Pinch of coarsely ground pepper
Pinch of nutmeg
Good pinch of salt

How to make it:
1. Make the roux in a normal manner and allow to cool.
2. Mix the milk into the roux until a smooth texture is obtained and bring to boiling point.
3. Meanwhile cut the veal into small cubes and stew with the butter, adding the onion, thyme, nutmeg, and seasoning. Allow to simmer for 2 hours on a low heat.
4. Pass through a strainer and coat the surface with butter to prevent the formation of skin.

Soubisse

This is more of a coulis than a sauce and it should be very white in colour. When it is made with béchamel it is much more smoother than when it is made with rice.

1. Slice 2 medium sized onions. Blanch them in boiling water and drain.
2. Place a good knob of butter in a saucepan and add the onions and cook.
3. Add to the pan 2½ cups of béchamel, a pinch of salt and pepper and a good pinch of caster sugar and cover tightly with lid. Place in the oven or on a low heat and cook gently.
4. Pass through a fine sieve. Reheat and finish the sauce by adding 2-3 knobs of butter and a good dash of cream.

Normande

Although this sauce is a perfect sauce for sole it also has a wide range of applications as a basis for other fish sauces.

How to make it:
Place 900 ml (1½ pints) of fish Veloute in a saucepan, half a cup of mushroom and mussels liquor, a cup of fish stock made from the bones of the soles and a few drops of lemon juice. Add 5 egg yolks and a cup of cream to the pan. Reduce quickly by one third and pass through a fine strainer. Finish by adding half a cup of double cream and 125g (4oz) of butter.

Mornay

This is a very popular sauce for fish, especially sole. When it is required for dishes other than fish use the same method of preparation but replace the fish cooking liquor with milk.

How to make it:
1. Add to 1 litre (1¾ pints) of Béchamel, a cup of cooking liquor from the fish with which the sauce is to be served.
2. Reduce by a third and then add 50g (2 oz) each of grated cheddar and Parmesan cheese.
3. Reheat for a few seconds mixing until the cheese is melted, then add 100g (3½ oz) of butter.

Lyonnaise

Sauce Lyonnaise is another name for "Brown Onion Sauce". This sauce could be served according to the requirements of the dish with which it is to be served or passed through a sieve.

How to make it:
1. In a saucepan heat 50g (2 oz) of butter. Add 250g (8 oz) finely chopped onion and cook until golden.
2. Add a cup of white wine and vinegar and reduce by two thirds.
3. Add a cup of demi-glace or brown sauce. Simmer gently for 5 minutes and pass through a sieve.

Genevoise

This sauce is also known as Genoise. Whether called Genevoise or Genoise all the classical authors and chefs agree upon one thing and that is the use of red wine in this sauce. This sauce is ideal served with salmon or trout.

What you need:
1kg /2½ lb salmon head
4 cups of fish stock
1¼ litre / 2 pints of red wine
200g / 7 oz butter
100g / 3½ oz carrots, finely chopped
1 medium onion, finely diced
30g / 1 oz parsley, finely chopped
1 Bay leaf
Sprig of thyme
Pinch of coarsley ground pepper
2 anchovy fillets or 1 tablespoon of anchovy essence

How to make it:
1. Heat 50g (2 oz) of butter in a saucepan with the onion, carrots, parsley, sprig of thyme and the bay leaf.
2. Add the salmon head and pepper and cook for 15 minutes.
3. Drain off the butter. Add the 1 litre (1¾ pints) of red wine and reduce by half.
4. Add 2 cups of fish stock and simmer for 1 hour.
5. Pass through a strainer into a clean pan and allow to rest for a few minutes.
6. Carefully remove any fat from the surface and add the rest of the red wine and the remainder of the fish stock.
7. Simmer, skim, reduce and strain. Finish by adding the anchovy fillets or essence and 150g (5 oz) of butter.

Cold related fish sauces

Mayonnaise

The best way to make a mayonnaise is to make it by hand, although most restaurants tend to use mixers and food processors. You need the yolks of two eggs, two tablespoons of white wine vinegar, 300ml (10 fl oz) olive oil and a pinch of salt.
Place the egg yolks, salt and vinegar into a mixing bowl and using a wire whisk beat the oil into the mixture a little at a time until you have incorporated it all.

Rouille

The easiest way to make this fiery sauce, especially if you are in a hurry is to get some mayonnaise, some crushed or finely chopped garlic, a pinch of cayenne pepper and mix them well together but I have evolved my own recipe as follows:
5 garlic cloves peeled, 3 red peppers (cooked, peeled and seeded), 2 teaspoons salt, 10 small green chillies, 1 teaspoon cayenne pepper, 500g (16 oz) mayonnaise, one egg yolk and 50g (2 oz) dried bread to be placed in the food processor. Blend together and chill.

Tartare

Tartare sauce is an excellent accompaniment to deep fried breaded fish such as scampi, cod and haddock. To make tartare sauce you first need mustard mayonnaise, this is basically English mustard powder blended in with mayonnaise. Add green olives, gherkins, capers, chives and parsley finely chopped. Mix the two together and you end up with sauce tartare.

Montpelier

This sauce is easy to make and is used for poached fish dishes.

1. In a saucepan, bring enough water to boil and blanch 100g (3 ½ oz) altogether, of tarragon, chives, parsley, chervil and watercress and 30g (1oz) of spinach for 30 seconds. Plunge them into cold water and squeeze out as much water as possible and place in a food processor.
2. Blanch 30g (1oz) of finely chopped shallots and place in the same food processor.
3. Add, 3 chopped gherkins, 10 capers, 5 anchovy fillets, 1 egg yolk, 4 hard boiled eggs and 4 oz (125g butter) to the food processor. Blend until smooth and then add 2-3 fl oz (75-90 ml) of olive oil.

Flavoured butter sauces

These sauces can easily be made by putting the ingredients and the butter which should be soft and not melted into a food processor. After blending spread the mixture onto cling film and roll to the thickness of a German sausage and chill. Slice before using for grilling or mixing in a sauce. Listed below are some of the most popular butter sauces.

Garlic butter

This is the most useful butter sauce and is used for making garlic bread. It can also be incorporated with other hot sauces or just used on its own.

250g / 8 oz unsalted butter softened and not melted
4 large cloves of garlic peeled and finely chopped
30g / 1oz parsley finely chopped
5ml / 1 teaspoon lemon juice
5ml / 1 teaspoon brandy
A good pinch of salt

Blend all the above listed ingredients together to form a smooth paste and chill.

Pistachio butter

Pound 150g (5 oz) pistachio nuts until fine and moisten with a few drops of water. Add 250g (9 oz) butter, mix in well and pass through a fine sieve.

Tarragon or parsley butter

This butter is good with any grilled or pan fried fish. The making of any other herb butters would be undertaken in exactly the same way.

250g / 8 oz unsalted butter softened but not melted
30g / 1oz fresh tarragon or parsley finely chopped
Juice of half lemon
Pinch of salt
Pinch of crushed black peppercorn

Mix all the above listed ingredients together to form a smooth texture and chill.

Coriander and pink pepper corn butter

250g / 8 oz unsalted butter softened but not melted
8g / 1 tablespoon pink peppercorns chopped
5ml / 1 teaspoon brandy
30g / 1oz freshly chopped coriander
Juice of half lemon
Pinch of salt
Pinch of crushed black peppercorn

Mix and blend all the above listed ingredients together to form a smooth texture and chill.

Butter sauce

Butter is made of fat globules from the cream of milk. It is a source of protein, minerals and vitamins "A & B" and so its main purpose in our diets is to provide energy. The butter sauce is one of the most perfect accompaniments for fish dishes which it enhances with its flavours.

Sauce au Beurre - English style

To make the butter sauce, just melt 50g (2 oz) butter in a saucepan until golden. Add 50g (2 oz) flour and mix well. Add 1 cup of water and bring to the boil. Add a dash of lemon juice and season with a little salt and some crushed black peppercorn and pour the sauce over your fish.

Devilled butter

Heat the required amount of butter till brown but not burnt. Add a pinch of Cayenne pepper, a pinch of black pepper, a pinch of curry powder and a pinch of ground ginger.

Green butter

Heat the required amount of butter till brown but not burnt. Add a good pinch of parsley, a dash of lemon juice (1 tablespoon), a little anchovy paste or essence and some salt and pepper. Mix thoroughly and use on your fish as required.

Horseradish butter

Heat the butter as above. Add 1 tablespoon grated horseradish and pound it with the butter and 1 tablespoon lemon juice adding it a drop at a time. Mix well and use the butter as required.

Maitre d'hotel butter

Cream the required butter in a frying pan over a low heat, add 2 tablespoons chopped parsley, 1 tablespoon chopped tarragon and chervil and mix in well. Add 1 teaspoon of lemon juice a drop at a time and season with a little salt and pepper. Spread the butter on a plate and chill until firm. Use as required.

Meunier butter (Noisette butter) or Lemon butter

Heat the required amount of butter till golden brown. Add some lemon juice and season with salt and pepper and use immediately.

Black butter sauce

Melt the butter in a saucepan till golden brown. Add the vinegar (for every 50g / 2 oz butter, use 1 tablespoon white wine vinegar) and cook for a further 2-3 minutes. In the variations 2 tablespoons of capers are also added.

Tarragon butter

Blanch 125g (4oz) of fresh tarragon leaves in a saucepan for 2 minutes and drain, refresh and squeeze dry. Pound the tarragon until fine then add 250g (9 oz) butter and mix well. Pass through a fine sieve and refrigerate until required.

Butter for snails

For about 50 snails, mix together 350g (13oz) butter, 25g (1 oz) finely chopped shallots, 1 clove of garlic crushed to a paste, 25g (1 oz) chopped parsley and a pinch of salt and pepper. Keep refrigerated until required.

Shrimp butter

Finely pound 150g (5 oz) of cooked shrimps to a fine paste, add butter in equal amount to the shrimp paste, mix and pass through a fine sieve.

Paprika butter

Take a paprika pepper and cook in butter with 1 finely chopped onion. Add 2 tablespoons of this paprika mixture to 250g (9 oz) softened butter. Mix in well and pass through a sieve.

Salad dressings

There is no point in buying good lettuce leaves such as cos, lolo roso, biande, curly endive, radicchio, young spinach leaves and rockets or purchasing and mixing some fresh herbs such as parsley, coriander, chives or basil for our salad if a wrong dressing is added to our ingredients, as this would spoil the taste.

The general rule for a good dressing is not to use malt vinegar but to use French wine vinegar. Cider or sherry vinegar and fruit vinegars are an absolute no, no. The oils to use for dressings are virgin olive oil, walnut oil, ground nut oil and soya oil. Sunflower oil is not my cup of tea and robustly flavoured oils such as sesame oil are not advised.

Basic dressing

The basic method of making a dressing is to use one part vinegar to three parts oil and add a pinch of salt and crushed black peppercorn. In some restaurants a pinch of mixed herbs is added to the dressing to make it more aromatic.

French dressing

90 ml / 6 tablespoons olive oil
30 ml / 2 tablespoons French wine vinegar
30 ml / 2 tablespoons juice of fresh lemon
1 yolk of egg
15 ml / 1 tablespoon whole grain/ Dijon mustard
Pinch of cracked black pepper
Seasoning

Place all the ingredients in a mixing bowl. Mix well using a wire whisk then store in a screw top jar or bottle and shake well each time before using as oil will separate.

STARTERS

Salads & cold starters

Salad consists of a mixture of edible leaves with some sort of dressing such as olive oil and vinegar. Although lettuce is the basic foundation of any salad we see some restaurants adding cooked and uncooked vegetables. French salads are composed of one vegetable only. In America they also use fruits and vegetables of all kinds. In Greece they use cheese and olives in their salads and in Italy, anything goes.

Salads can be divided into two types and these are referred to as simple or compound. The differences are as follows:-

Simple salads are raw and always accompany hot roasts.

Compound salads consist of cooked vegetables and always accompany cold roasts.

Crab and avocado salad (Austrian)

I have to admit I love avocados and I think they go very well with shellfish.

Serves 6

What you need:

450g / 1 lb mixed white and brown crabmeat
3 ripe avocados
60 ml / 4 tablespoons mayonnaise
30 ml / 2 tablespoons juice of freshly squeezed lemon
1 tablespoon mixed chopped parsley and chives
A wedge of lemon
A pinch of salt and pepper

How to make it:

1. Cut each avocado in half, de-stone, peel and with a sharp knife slice the avocado side up and make a fan shape at the edge of your serving plate.
2. Mix together the mayonnaise, lemon juice, chopped herbs and seasoning then mix well with the crab meat.
3. Spoon out the mixture on top of the avocado and garnish with a lemon wedge.

Seafood salad

Seafood salad is regarded as being a very British salad because all the fish used are readily available around the shores of Britain.

Serves 4

What you need:
225g / 8 oz squid cleaned, washed and sliced in rings
110g / 4 oz shelled cooked cockles
450g / 1 lb mussels or 110g / 4 oz cooked
4 scallops removed from the shell and washed
2 spring onions
1 medium carrot
1 celery stalk
French dressing

How to make it:
1. Place the scallops in a pan of white wine vinegar. Bring to the boil and simmer for five minutes then remove using a slotted spoon.
2. Place the squid in the same pan and simmer until it starts to curl at the edges then remove with the slotted spoon.
3. Add the cockles and mussels to the bowl of squid and scallops and mix well.
4. Trim and slice the spring onions lengthwise into ribbons. Place them in ice-cold water as this makes them curl up like flowers. Do the same with the carrot peel. Then slice the celery hearts and place in the iced water.
5. Place all your fish and vegetables together. Mix well and add some French dressing (see page 52) and serve immediately. Garnish with chopped parsley.

Cocktail de Crevette (French)
Prawn cocktail

This is the easiest of all salads to make and it only takes minutes. Large Mediterranean prawns should be served in their shells, along with a lemon wedge and a finger bowl. For the convenience of customers, prawns are shelled and are served with buttered brown bread and cayenne pepper in many restaurants.

Serves 2

What you need:
1 small heart of iceberg lettuce washed and shredded
2 cups of peeled prawns defrosted, washed and drained from water
75 ml / 5 tablespoons mayonnaise
15 ml / 1 tablespoon tomato puree / ketchup
3 lemon wedges
5 ml / 1 teaspoon vinegar
1 teaspoon cayenne pepper
A pinch of salt

How to make it:
Arrange the lettuce in the centre of a plate or a cocktail glass. Place the prawns on top to form a pyramid. Mix all the ingredients with the exception of the cayenne pepper, with the juice of one lemon wedge. Pour the sauce over the prawn cocktail and drizzle the cayenne pepper over the sauce. Serve with a lemon wedge.

Insalata di Mare (Italian)

Every region of Italy has invented their own recipe for this seafood salad. This recipe can be kept in a tight screw-top container for some time.

Use equal quantities of cooked mussels, cockles, squid rings, tuna and prawns (if using anchovies, only use a few because of their saltiness) and mix them together in a bowl. Season with salt and pepper, some crushed black peppercorn, a few cloves of garlic and some oregano. Add enough olive oil, white wine vinegar and lemon juice to cover. Refrigerate for at least one hour before use. Insalata di Mer should always be served on a bed of shredded lettuce.

Salade Nicoise (French)

The original salad nicoise is equal quantities of French beans, diced potatoes and tomato quarters, decorated with stoned olives, capers, small (a variety of fish), anchovy fillets and seasoned with only oil and vinegar. But, modern style cookery has changed all that.

1 tuna steak or 225g/ 8 oz can of tuna in brine
1 hard boiled egg
20g /1 oz black olives
50g / 2 oz or 2 boiled new potatoes, quartered
2 anchovy fillets
20g / 1 oz capers
50g / 2 oz green beans, cooked
25g / 1 oz or 1 fresh tomato, quartered
20g / 1 oz red onion, sliced in rings
100g / 3½ oz mixed leaves
50g / 2 oz bread dough
45 ml / 3 tablespoons French dressing

Place the leaves in the centre of the plate, add the olives, capers and beans then place the tuna on top and the onion rings on top of the tuna. Now place the anchovy fillets crosswise on top of the onion rings. Arrange the tomato, potato, bread dough and egg around the plate and drizzle with some French dressing (see page 47) to serve.

Pickled herring and apple salad (English)

This is the only summer salad that most people have as a main course. People who like pickled herrings, like my mother, go to any lengths to get their hands on these fish and according to her, they are heavenly even on their own.

Serves 6

What you need:
6 pickled herrings, all sliced onions removed from inside and unrolled and cut into 2½ cm / 1 inch chunks.
3 apples, cored and quartered, with the skins on and cut into little 1 cm chunks.
1 iceberg or Cos lettuce finely shredded.
1 tablespoon finely chopped parsley
150 ml / ¼ pint sour cream
1 lemon quartered
Pinch of sesame seeds
Pinch of black pepper

How to make it:
Place everything into a bowl and mix (except lettuce, sesame seeds and parsley). Arrange the shredded lettuce in the centre of the plate. Place the mixture on the top and garnish with lemon wedge and a sprinkle of parsley and sesame seeds. Serve with a hot crust bread bun and butter.

Mosaic of Cod, Smoked haddock and Pink Salmon Terrine

This is one of the loveliest ways to enjoy terrine, but one of the most fiddly to make. Most people like to buy this dish ready made as it is often considered to be time consuming to prepare. Nevertheless, it is fun to sometimes create a visually attractive or unusual dish. This terrine, which is made from three different fish, is certainly striking in appearance as well as excellent tasting. The final effect is three different coloured layers with spots of coloured square mosaic effects in-between and when it is served, what you get is a beautiful patterned shaped terrine on your plate.

You will need: a food processor and a small rectangular terrine dish 11½ x 9 cm (4½ x 3½ inches) and 5-7½ cm (2-3 inches) deep.

For the white part:
225 g / 8 oz cod fillet, skinned and diced finely
30g / 1 oz butter, a good knob
1 clove garlic, finely crushed
½ medium onion, finely diced
The juice of ½ a lemon
2 anchovy fillets, chopped
A pinch of black pepper seasoning

How to make it:
Pan fry the onion and garlic in the butter over a medium heat. Add the cod and stir fry until cooked. Place in the processor along with the rest of the ingredients and blend. Refrigerate to firm up slightly.

For the yellow part:
1 smoked haddock fillet, approx. 140 g / 5 oz skinned and picked
½ a small onion, sliced
Pinch of crushed black peppercorn
Dash of Tabasco
The juice of ½ a lemon
150 ml / ¼ pint milk
1-2 bay leaves, Pinch of turmeric (optional for added colour)

How to make it:
Place the haddock, milk, onion, black pepper and the bay leaves in the frying pan and poach for a few minutes. Lift out the haddock and place in the food processor and puree (with a pinch of turmeric, if you want more colour) adding the rest of the ingredients. Let the mixture cool to firm up.

For the pink part:
1 pink salmon steak (approx.140 g / 5 oz)
½ small onion sliced
1– 2 bay leaves
150 ml / ¼ pint dry white wine
A pinch of crushed black pepper corn

How to make it:
Poach the salmon in a frying pan together with the wine, onion, bay leaves and peppercorn for a few minutes until cooked. Strain, skin and de-bone. Puree in the food processor and refrigerate to firm up.

For the mosaic:
4 carrots, peeled and shaved to a cylinder pen shape and then cooked until softened.
4 asparagus tips, head and tailed, and cooked briefly.

Lightly oil the terrine dish. Place all the cod mixture in the dish and press down. Lay, one carrot, one asparagus next to each other and repeat. Now, place the salmon on top and press down. Lay one carrot and one asparagus next to each other and repeat. Now, place the haddock puree on top and press down. Chill again in a refrigerator for several hours. Run a sharp knife around the dish, shake from side to side to loosen and then turn upside down onto a plate. Slice and serve with melba toast.

Poached turbot Guacamole
with avocado sauce

Serves 4

What you need:
2 avocado pears, cut in ½, remove stones and scoop out flesh
1 turbot, poached, cooled down and cut into 4 slices
1 medium onion grated
Juice of ½ a lemon
A pinch of ground ginger or 1 teaspoon of freshly chopped ginger
60ml / 4 tablespoons of olive oil
A pinch of salt and cayenne pepper

How to make it:
1. Puree the avocado. Mix in the lemon juice and pass through a fine sieve.
2. Rub the grated onion into the avocado puree. Season with salt, cayenne pepper and a pinch of dried ginger.
3. Gradually beat the oil into the avocado until the mixture is the consistency of mayonnaise.
4. Place the turbot slices on a serving dish and top with a little chilled avocado sauce.

Calamari salad (South African)

Serves 4

1. Take 450g (1 lb) frozen squid, defrost, clean, wash and slice into 1 cm rings and cut the tentacles into bite size pieces. Place in a pan of boiling water to curl. Remove and cool and place in a bowl with the juice and the rinds of one lemon to marinate.
2. In another bowl (preferably glass) place the shredded heart of an iceberg lettuce with 2 chopped tomatoes, one quarter cucumber diced in chunks, 2 radishes quartered, 2 hard boiled eggs quartered and a dozen pitted black olives.
3. Add the squid rings to the glass bowl, mix and drizzle with some French dressing.

Smoked haddock pâté (Smoky pâté)

This is a quick and easy pâté to make, which becomes even more so if you use a food processor.

Serves 8

What you need:
4 smoked haddocks skinned and flaked
175 - 200g / 6-7 oz unsalted butter melted
Juice of 2 fresh lemons
Grated rind of one lemon
Pinch of ground black pepper
1 tablespoon finely chopped parsley

How to make it:
Place the flesh of the haddock in the food processor and blend slowly adding the butter until it is all used up. Add the lemon juice, lemon rind and pepper and blend for a further 30 seconds. Remove and place in a bowl to chill. Scoop out the pâté and place on a serving plate. Garnish with some chopped parsley and serve with either finger or melba toast.

Taramasalata (Smoked cod's roe pâté)

What I don't understand, when I go to a Greek restaurant, is why taramasalata is dyed a hideous pink colour and over salted rather than being pale with a delicate flavour. My version, as well as being much cheaper to make, is utterly delicious.

Serves 8

What you need:
4 oz / 110g smoked cod's roe skinned
30 ml / 2 tablespoons milk
½ small onion chopped in quarters
1 clove garlic crushed
2 medium slices of white bread
Juice of half lemon
150 ml / ¼ pint olive oil
Pinch of black pepper (no salt is needed)
Black olives

How to make it:
Put the cod's roe in cold water to soak for 30 minutes. Remove and then leave for the excess water to drip out. Remove the crust from the bread and soak in the milk for a few minutes until a spongy paste has been achieved. Squeeze out any excess milk and place in a food processor. Add the cod, onion, garlic and pepper and process until smooth. As the machine is running add the oil a little at a time, then add the lemon juice. Remove pâté, place on a serving dish and garnish with black olives and serve with either melba toast or pitta bread.

Hot starters and soups

To amuse the palate small pre dinner snacks known as "amuse-gueule" by caterers are served in most restaurants. These are a very important part of a meal for a very hungry person and may even be considered the most memorable part.

Etouffee

This is a New Orleans recipe which requires long slow cooking if your prawns and crab are raw and unshelled and your stock not ready. If however you have the time and the patience it makes a delicious starter.

Serves 6

What you need:
900g / 2 lb shelled prawns, cooked
450g / 1 lb crab meat
1.25 litres / 2 pints fish stock and roux mixed (see recipe page 37)
45ml / 3 tablespoons olive oil
2 onions, fairly large, peeled and finely chopped
4 celery stalks, finely chopped
6 spring onions, roughly chopped
2 tablespoons parsley, finely chopped
2 red pimentos, seeded and finely chopped
A pinch of cayenne pepper
A pinch of black pepper
A pinch of salt

How to make it:
Fry the all the vegetables in a frying pan with the exception of the spring onion in olive oil until tender. Add the crabmeat and prawns and fry for a further 2 minutes. Add the fish stock and let it simmer to reduce, then add the spring onion and parsley and let it cook for a further 2 minutes. Add the seasoning and serve immediately.

Tandoori prawns

Most people from Northern India with their own private tandoori ovens create an array of astonishing dishes. These dishes can be created just as successfully using a frying pan or wok.

Serves 4

What you need:
675g / 1 ½ lbs un-shelled prawns or 450g / 1 lb peeled prawns
3 tablespoons cumin seeds, pan fried and roasted dry (in no oil)
600ml / 1 pint natural yogurt
2 cloves of garlic, finely crushed
2 tablespoons ginger, freshly grated
2 tablespoons coriander, finely chopped
1 ½ tablespoons garam masala
Knob of butter
Pinch of salt and pepper

How to make it:
1. Mix all the ingredients in a bowl.
2. Add the prawns and if they are un-shelled, longitudinally with a sharp knife loosen and remove the shells, and marinate for 30- 60 minutes.
3. Remove the prawns with a slotted spoon, shaking well to remove any of the marinade.
4. Melt the butter in a large frying pan and stir fry the prawns for a few minutes. Traditionally, tandoori dishes are served with naan bread rather than rice.

Tempura

This is a marvellous Japanese dish and a famous Japanese speciality which is encased in tempura batter and served with a special dip. The host, chef or cook must be very patient, skilled and heat resistant to keep cooking the food as you and your guests keep replenishing your plates as rapidly as you empty them.

Serves 4

What you need:
12 shelled, tail on prawns
20 whitebait
16 shelled mussels
4 small fish fillets
Vegetable oil for frying or sesame oil
Any 4 vegetables cut into 2.5 cm / 1 inch long pieces such as: baby corn cobs, broccoli or cauliflower floret's, blanched French beans, bamboo shoots, lotus roots, seaweed, celery, mushrooms, green pimentos, mange tout.

.

For the batter mix: Break one large egg in a bowl and stir gently until both the white and yolk are well mixed. Add 120ml (4 fl oz) water and mix again, then sift in 120g (4oz) flour, mixing again lightly.

For the Tempura dip or sauce: mix 2 tablespoons grated ginger, 180 ml (6 fl oz) soy sauce, 60 ml (2 fl oz) Mirin, Japanese rice wine, a good pinch of hana katsuo (dried Bonito flakes) or grated horseradish.

How to make it:
In a clean wok or deep fryer heat the oil until hot but not smoky. Dip the fish into the tempura batter and fry for one minute until golden (little batches at a time). Similarly fry the vegetables. Dry on absorbent paper and serve with the tempura sauce and rice which should be boiled and sticky.

Ragoût de Fruits de Mer
Serves 2

This dish, using good-sized prawns, makes a great main course or can be served as a luxury starter. It is very easy to make and almost any shellfish can be used.

225g / 8 oz unshelled prawns
16 clean bearded mussels
1 medium sized onion, diced
Knob of butter
2 cloves of garlic peeled and chopped
4 fresh tomatoes, chopped or (250g / 8 oz tin chopped tomato)
1 tablespoon sugar
1 tablespoon flour
1 glass dry white wine
Pinch of thyme
Pinch of salt and pepper

Fry the onion and garlic in butter in a deep sided frying pan until golden. Add the tomatoes, sugar and thyme and season well cooking for 5-7 minutes. Add a pinch of flour, shake, then add the wine and mussels and cover the pan. When mussels open add the prawns and cook for a further 2 minutes. Serve immediately.

Frito Misto Mare

This is the only starter which can be shared and it is known as Italian fish and chips without the chips. Most Italian restaurants are getting it wrong, why? Because, when you ask for this dish, you never get what you are supposed to (a minimum of three kinds of fish - prawns, red mullet and squid). You usually end up getting deep fried whitebait, fried scampi and fried squid.

The ingredients can either be dipped in milk and flour before frying in good quality olive or sunflower oil, or they can be battered or just dusted with flour before frying. There is no need to use a deep fryer. A large capacious frying pan or a wok will do but use a generous supply of oil. Serve immediately with plenty of lemon wedges, bread and garlic butter sauce.

Prawns peri-peri

During the month I worked at 'Carolinas', a South African restaurant in the North east of England, I developed a close relationship with prawns and a sauce called peri-peri. Unlike curry dishes "prawns peri-peri" washes down very well with wine.

This dish from Mozambique originally came from Portugal, but no matter where it came from, it has many versions and here is one of them.

Serves 2-3

What you need:
450g / 1 lb unshelled fresh uncooked prawns
1 teaspoon dried or 1 tablespoon fresh chillies finely chopped
½ glass of dry white wine
Dash of brandy
1 clove garlic finely crushed
Pinch or two of salt
30 ml / 2 tablespoons or more of olive oil for marinade
15 ml / 1 tablespoon lemon juice

How to make it:
Heat enough oil to coat and cook the prawns for 3-4 minutes in a frying pan. Add half of the chillies to flavour and fry for a further 2 minutes. Add a good pinch of salt and allow to cool for an hour. Fry the garlic and the remainder of the chillies briefly in a little oil. Add the wine and lemon juice, bring to the boil and simmer for 2 minutes. Flame with the brandy and pour over the prawns in the marinade. This dish can be served with naan bread, rice and salad.

Fricassée de Crevettes
Serves 2-3

The Fricassée differs from Blanquette in as much as the meat, in our case fish and garnish, are cooked directly in its sauce.

What you need:
750g / 1 ½ lbs fresh shelled prawns
Knob of butter
1 glass sweet white wine
1 glass water
1 glass single cream
1 celery stick, chopped
2 carrots, chopped
4 shallots, chopped
Dash of brandy
Pinch of tarragon and chervil
Dash of Tabasco
Pinch of salt and pepper
Plain flour

How to make it:
Pan fry the shallots, carrots and celery in the butter until softened. Remove the heads and shells from the prawns and add them to the pan (not the prawns) with a little plain flour. Stir in the brandy, wine and water and simmer for 10 minutes before adding the cream. Simmer for a further minute and then strain through a sieve into another pan and throw away the debris. Add the chervil and peeled prawns and cook on a low heat for 5-6 minutes. Season with salt, pepper, and Tabasco and serve immediately, garnishing with the tarragon. (Serve with boiled rice if using as a main course.)

Fillets of Brill with pink peppercorn Sabayon

This fish dish is difficult to sell in fish restaurants because Brill is not that well known. It is however a marvellous flat fish and cheaper than turbot. If you cannot find Brill consider using plaice or sole, both of which are very popular.

Serves 2

What you need:
4 Brill fillets approximately 90g / 3 oz each
600ml / 1 pint fish stock, (see page 37)
1 glass Noilly Prat (a sweet vermouth)
3 egg yolks
Knob of butter melted
1 teaspoon pink peppercorn
Pinch of salt and pepper

How to make it:
1. Place the fish stock, Noilly Prat and salt and pepper for reduction in a frying pan. Bring to the boil on a low heat and simmer to reduce the sauce. Remove from the heat.
2. Brush the fillets with melted butter and place under the grill to cook.
3. Whisk the stock reduction into the egg yolks. Reheat until hot, remove pan from stove and mix in the pink peppercorns.
4. Place the fillets in the centre of the plate and pour the sauce over the fish.

Fried squid with an ink sauce

The ink sauce is made of the ink in which the squid screens itself from its enemies. As one ink sac produces a few drops, we will have enough ink to colour and flavour our sauce.

Serves 4

What you need:
450g / 1 lb squid. For cleaning and removing the ink sac, see page 19
1 medium onion, finely chopped
2 cloves of garlic, crushed
45 ml / 3 tablespoons ground nut oil
250g / ½ lb plain flour
1 tablespoon bread crumbs
Good pinch of chopped parsley
Good dash of brandy
30g / 3 oz fresh tomato, peeled, deseeded and then chopped
Salt and pepper for seasoning

How to make it:
1. Mix the sacs with two tablespoons of water in a bowl. Slice the squid into rings, coat with the seasoned flour and then fry in the hot oil, in batches. Once fried, remove with a perforated spoon to a serving dish.
2. In the same frying pan, fry the onion and garlic for 1 or 2 minutes. Add the tomato and fry for a further 2 minutes. Add the brandy and the strained black ink and reduce the liquid.
3. Finally add the chopped parsley and breadcrumbs. Season, and serve immediately on four plates.

Grilled sardines with a shallot dressing

This is a dish that needs no expertise. You just grill or barbecue 8 sardines.

For the sauce; all you have to do is combine or mix in a frying pan on a low heat the following ingredients, - 60 ml (2 fl oz) of olive oil, 15 ml (½ fl oz) white wine vinegar, 30g (1 oz) freshly chopped shallots, 15 ml (½ oz) freshly chopped parsley and some salt and pepper. Pour the sauce over the sardines and serve.

Sautéed scallops with chicory and Noilly Prat

Scallops go well with any sweet vermouth and Noilly Prat is a divine variety. Scallops are also nice baked in their own shells or just pan fried with a little butter. The recipe below is one of my favourites.

Serves 4

What you need:
8-12 good sized scallops, each sliced into three rounds and corals separated
450ml / 15 fl oz fish stock, see recipe on page 37
2 knobs of butter
90g / 3 oz chicory, cut into thin strips 2½cm / 1 inch long
60 ml / 2 fl oz Noilly Prat
150ml / 5 fl oz double cream
Salt and pepper

How to make it:
1. Pour the fish stock and Noilly Prat into a saucepan boiling on a high heat in order to reduce the liquid by two thirds, then add chicory and cream and reduce still further. Whisk the butter into the sauce and season. Divide the sauce onto 4 plates.
2. Brush a frying pan with a little oil and place on the stove to heat. Put the scallops into the pan turning over almost immediately. Cook for a further few seconds and remove and place on top of the chicory sauce.

Oysters with Beurre Blanc and Spinach

To make this dish one has to feel the urge for creating it. One of the most daunting parts of learning about classic French fish cookery is that when it comes to oysters, especially with this dish, the oysters are hardly cooked at all.

Serves 4

What you need:
16 oysters, thoroughly washed
16 spinach leaves, stalks removed and washed
150g / 5 oz unsalted butter
8 shallots or 1 medium onion, finely chopped
4 glasses of water
1 glass white wine
1 glass white wine vinegar
Salt and pepper to season if required

How to make it:
1. Steam cook the oysters for 4-5 minutes. If you don't have a steamer, boil some water in a saucepan, place a plate on top of the saucepan, put your oysters on the plate and cover them with another plate. The oysters may take longer to cook using this method but the same result is achieved. Remove the oysters and keep the juice that comes out of them.
2. Put the shallots, vinegar, wine and water, along with the juice from the oysters in a small pan and simmer to reduce, till one glass of liquid is left.
3. Steam the spinach leaves for 2 minutes.
4. Remove the reduced liquid from the heat and add the butter, whisking in a little at a time.
5. Remove the oysters from their shells. Place a folded spinach leaf in the bottom of each shell and place the shells on a suitable serving dish.
6. Now, place the dish under the grill to warm up. Put the oysters back into their shells and pour the beurre blanc over each one. (Season if required.) Warm again briefly under the grill and serve with a bottle of Chablis.

Escargots à la Bourguignonne– Snails

Go to any French restaurant and snails are on the menu. English people are beginning to have a taste for this pre- dinner dish.

1. Push into the inside of each empty snail shell, a small piece of snail garlic parsley butter, followed by the cooked snail and then close off the entrance to the shell with more of the garlic butter, packing in as much as possible.
2. Arrange on a dish or special snail dish with the stuffed ends upward. Pour a little water over the bottom of the dish.
3. Sprinkle the butter ends with a few fine white breadcrumbs and place in a pre- heated oven for 5-6 minutes.

Grenouilles Sautées aux Fines Herbes– Frogs

Once again when you present a menu with frogs on many customers in restaurants still look astonished. However frog dishes are increasing in popularity and are even being served in Italian restaurants.

Frog's legs, come clean and frozen so, all you have to do is to defrost them, season them with salt and pepper and marinate for an hour with a little lemon juice and olive oil, crushed garlic and some chopped parsley. When required, just shallow fry them in butter on all sides, drain and serve with some salad leaves and garnish with more chopped parsley and lemon wedges.

Calamari

Squid makes a beautiful starter, especially when it is ringed and soaked in milk, dusted with flour or battered and deep fried. Serve it with some leaves and some lemon wedges and it is heavenly. These days you can buy cleaned or ringed squid from your local superstore or fishmongers.

SOUPS

Shellfish bisque

This is a soup using the shells, which give the bisque its grainy texture, as well as the meat of the prawns, crabs and lobster. - In restaurants, everything gets used and nothing is wasted. Something that is not good for one recipe can be used elsewhere. For example leek tops can be used for making stock and garnishing soup, hard dried cheese for gratin, old leftover bread for croutons, and vegetable skins and pairings for soups etc. - So when it comes to bisque, keep the meat and use it in salads etc.

What you need:
700g / 1 ½ lbs shells, heads, cavities of prawns, crabs, etc.
1 large onion, chopped finely
2 carrots, peeled and chopped
2 celery sticks, chopped
90g / 3 oz butter
Dash of brandy
4 tomatoes
1 tablespoon tomato puree
1 glass dry vermouth
2 bay leaves
1.4 litres / 2 ½ pints fish stock, and not stock cubes
⅔ cup of rice
120ml / 4 fl oz cream
Juice of ½ lemon freshly squeezed
A pinch of salt, pepper and cayenne pepper

How to make it:

1. Place the butter together with the onion, carrots, celery and bay leaves in a saucepan and cook till they change colour.
2. Remove any stomach sacs from the shellfish and cut the shells up as much as possible. Add to the saucepan and pound them into the vegetables with a rolling pin.
3. Pour in the brandy and add the tomatoes, tomato puree and vermouth and reduce.
4. Add the fish stock and rice to the pan. Bring to the boil and simmer for 20 minutes.
5. Remove the thick shells and the fish meat from the pan. Liquidise the remaining ingredients including the shells to a point that the shells are no bigger than a fingernail.
6. Pass the soup through a conical strainer, then twice through a fine strainer.
7. Add the cream, lemon juice and cayenne pepper.
8. Season with salt and pepper and serve immediately.

Soupe de poissons (fish soup)

This is the sort of soup you find in every coastal restaurant in France. The aim of using the liquidiser is to use the shells and heads as well as everything else. Almost any fish except the oily ones can be used. The ideal fish are conger, eel, skate, cod, dog fish and shark etc. These are normally mixed with some cheap white fish such as pollack, whiting, gurnard or grey mullet.

What you need:
900-1300g / 2-3 lb filleted fish
1.7 litres / 3 pints water
159 ml / 5 fl oz olive oil
1 large onion, peeled and chopped roughly
3 celery stalks, roughly chopped
1 large head of leek, roughly chopped
1 large fennel, roughly chopped
5 garlic cloves, finely chopped
4 large tomatoes, quartered
11 tablespoons tomato puree
The peel of one orange
½ a red pepper, peeled
2 bay leaves
A pinch of saffron
A pinch of cayenne pepper
A pinch of salt and pepper

How to make it:
Cook the vegetables in the olive oil in a large saucepan over a high heat until tender. Add the tomato puree, orange peel, bay leaves, saffron and the fish fillets. Stir, then add the water. Bring to boil and simmer for 40 minutes. Now liquidise and pass the soup through a strainer. Place the soup back in the pan and heat up. Add the cayenne pepper and season with salt and pepper to taste. Serve with fried bread covered with Parmesan cheese floating on top of the soup.

Mussel and leek soup

This is the only soup which smells as good as it tastes. In fact this exotic fish soup, with the aroma of saffron, is something that you first eat with your nose - it smells heavenly!- before enjoying the wonderful taste.

What you need:
11.4 kg / 3 lb mussels washed and scraped clean. (Discarding the open ones.)
240g / 8 oz leeks, chopped
90g / 3 oz butter
1 glass dry white wine
45g / 1½ oz flour
450 ml / 15 ½ fl oz fish stock, see page 37
½ a glass of double cream
1 onion, finely chopped
A good pinch of saffron
Seasoning

How to make it:
1. Place the mussels and a dash of the wine in a saucepan, cover and cook for 5 minutes, shaking the pan until all the mussels have opened, then strain the juice into a bowl.
2. In a saucepan, place the butter, onion, leeks and seasoning and cook on a high heat for 3 minutes.
3. Once, the vegetables are glazed, add the remaining wine and let it reduce by half, then add the flour and stir until smooth.
4. Mix the mussel juice with the fish stock and gradually add it to the pan. Bring to a simmer and add the saffron. Leave to cook for 30 minutes.
5. Whilst still simmering, pull out the mussels and discard half of the shells. Liquidise the soup and strain through a sieve. Add the cream and the mussels and serve immediately.

Canton Corn Fish soup

This is a Cantonese soup and it comes from Canton in south-east China. There is an old Chinese saying: "Die in Lui-Chow, but eat in Kwang-Chow". This is because the first is famous for its coffins and the second for its excellent cuisine. As would be expected, seafood plays an important part in the cooking of southern China. Prawns, abalone, scallops, lobster and crab are heavily flavoured either with ginger or onion or both, and they are either stir fried or steamed unless used for making soup.

What you need:
450g / 1 lb white fish such as filleted cod or
5 ml / 1 teaspoon fresh ginger, finely chopped
Dash of sherry
900 ml / 1½ pints water
225 g / 8 oz tin sweet corn, drained
A good dash of olive oil
1 spring onion or shallots, chopped
A good pinch of cornstarch or cornflour, dissolved
  in 1 tablespoon water
Seasoning

How to make it:
1. In a heat proof dish place the fish, sherry and ginger with a generous pinch of salt and leave to marinate for 10 minutes.
2. Place the dish in a steamer for 5-6 minutes, remove from the heat and mash and set aside.
3. Pour the water into a large saucepan and bring to the boil.
4. Add the sweet corn, oil and a pinch of salt and simmer for a further 2 minutes.
5. Add the cornflour mixture and stir until the soup thickens.
6. Add the fish and cook for a further minute.
7. Pour into the soup bowl. Sprinkle with the spring onion and serve.

Bouillabaisse à la Marseillaise

This, the most famous of all fish soups, is made chiefly in the South of France. It is a thick fish stew which should include a very wide range of different kinds of fish. For this reason, a large quantity is normally made.

For the fish:
The fish I use for this recipe are monkfish, conger eel or eel, red mullet, crab, whiting, lobster, gurnet, fielas, sea bass and sole.
Divide the fish into two according to the type of flesh (i.e. soft and firm) Clean and cut the fish into thick slices. Place those with firm flesh into a saucepan and keep the soft ones in a separate bowl.

1kg / 2 lb mixed fish
1 large onion, finely chopped
1 leek, sliced
1 clove garlic, crushed
2 tomatoes, peeled, seeded and sliced
A sprig of parsley
A sprig of tarragon
30 – 45 ml / 2-3 tablespoons good virgin olive oil
1 glass of dry white wine, preferably Chardonnay
2 bay leaves
Saffron dissolved in 1 teaspoon of water or a little sprig of dried saffron
 A pinch of salt and pepper

1. Place the firm fish in a saucepan over a moderate heat. Arrange all the vegetables, herbs and spices on top of the fish. Add the oil, wine and enough water or fish stock to cover both the fish and the vegetables and bring to the boil quickly cooking for a further 8-10 minutes.
2. Add the soft fish and boil for a further 5 minutes, then simmer for 1 minute.
3. Place a toasted slice of bread at the bottom of every serving bowl and pour the fish liquid over the toast.
4. Serve the mixture of the fish separately. You can ignore the vegetables.

Conger eel soup
Soupe aux anguilles

This is a soup with a difference. Flour, butter and cream are used in the preparation of this kind of soup.

Serves 6

What you need:
450 g / 1lb conger eel or eel, cleaned and cut into small pieces
1 large onion, finely sliced
A good knob of butter
A pinch of mixed herbs or 2 tablespoons freshly chopped herbs
1 lemon rind
Juice of ½ the lemon
2 tablespoons flour
A good dash of cream
Fish stock or water, enough to cover the ingredients
Salt and pepper for seasoning

How to make it:
1. Melt the butter in a saucepan. Add the onion and eel and gently fry without browning them.
2. Add water or stock and bring to the boil. Add the herbs, lemon juice, rind and seasoning and simmer until the eel is cooked. Strain and keep the sauce in another saucepan.
3. Blend the flour with the cream and stir into the liquid. Bring to boil.
4. Add the pieces of eel and simmer for a further minute and serve.

MAIN COURSES

The connoisseur's guide
To
Universal classic fish dishes

Seafood paella

This rice dish is just fascinating. Add some vegetables and it is known as vegetable paella. Add shrimps, mussels and monkfish 7-8 minutes before the end of cooking time and the dish you end up with is known as seafood paella.

Serves 4-6

What you need:

450g / 1 lb mixture of shelled mussels, shelled shrimps, and skinned and boned monkfish
1 aubergine, trimmed and diced in ½ cm. cubes
250 g / 9 oz courgettes, topped, tailed and sliced
100 ml / 3½ fl oz olive oil
1 large onion, peeled and finely chopped
2 garlic cloves, crushed
100 g / 4 oz carrots, peeled and diced into 1 cm. cubes
2 peppers, red and green, seeded and roughly chopped
450 g / 1 lb long grain rice, washed
1.2 litres / 2 pints water or fish stock
½ teaspoon saffron powder
Sprig of thyme
1 bay leaf
200 g / 7 oz tomato concassee or tin of chopped tomato
100 g / 4 oz peas
Salt and pepper

How to make it:

1. Place the courgettes and aubergines in different colanders and lightly sprinkle with salt and pepper and leave for at least one hour.
2. Fry the onion and garlic in the olive oil for a few minutes.
3. Add the carrots and cook for 2-4 minutes.
4. Add the peppers, aubergines and courgettes to the frying pan and cook for a further 5 minutes.
5. Add the rice and stir to coat with the oil.
6. Add the stock or water. Season with salt, pepper, saffron, thyme and the bay leaf. Bring to the boil and then simmer for 25-30 minutes.
7. Add the fish, tomato and peas. Cook for a further 7-8 minutes and serve.

Spaghetti Marinara

Any pasta is as good as spaghetti when it comes to seafood. It is a matter of choice. This recipe is my favourite recipe from Australia. A starter portion is enough to keep me going for the whole day even though I am not Australian.

Serves 6-8

What you need:
900 g / 2 lb mixed fish including, scallops, cockles, prawns, oysters and lobster meat
450 g / 1 lb spaghetti
60 ml / 4 tablespoons olive oil
2 cloves garlic, sliced
200 g / 7 oz tomato, freshly chopped
1 tablespoon tomato puree
1 glass dry red wine
1 pinch of dried oregano or 1 teaspoon freshly chopped
1 pinch of dried parsley or 1 teaspoon freshly chopped
A good pinch of salt and pepper

How to make it:
1. Sauté the shelled fish and pieces of lobster meat in a frying pan in medium hot oil.
2. Remove the fish from the pan and add the garlic. Sauté until golden.
3. Add the tomato, tomato puree, wine, herbs and salt and pepper to the pan. Cook rapidly uncovered for 15 minutes until thickened. (add a little water if the sauce becomes too dry).
4. Add fish and reheat gently.
5. Meanwhile, bring the water to the boil in a saucepan and add a pinch of salt and a dash of oil. Place the spaghetti in the boiling water and cook it to your liking. Serve immediately with the fish sauce.

Fisherman's pie

Around the coast of the Caspian sea, people with large families have the following tradition. "To feed their families on a healthy diet consisting of food dishes that are both simple and quick to make, economical on the purse and delicious to eat." Fisherman's pie is such a dish.

Serves 4-6

What you need:
450 g / 1 lb hake, kingklip fillet, or any firm fleshed fish
5 medium potatoes, cooked and peeled
60 ml / 4 tablespoons milk
Knob of butter
1 large egg
2 large, hard boiled eggs, sliced
125 g / ¼ lb button mushrooms, fried in butter
Pinch of sugar
Juice of one lemon
15 ml / 1 tablespoon freshly chopped parsley
45 ml / 3 tablespoons grated cheddar cheese
300 ml / 1½ cups béchamel or white sauce (see recipe 44
Salt and pepper for seasoning

How to make it:
1. Bake the fish in a pre-heated oven with the sugar, lemon juice, butter, salt and pepper for no more than 20 minutes.
2. Place the potato in a saucepan with a little salt. Cover with water and bring to the boil until tender. Mash with a little milk, butter and the raw egg.
3. Stir the fish flakes into the béchamel along with the hard-boiled eggs, parsley and mushrooms and pour into an ovenproof dish.
4. Cover with the creamed potatoes and sprinkle with the grated cheese and refrigerate.
5. Place the dish back in the oven or under the grill to brown the surface before serving.

Baked hake Portuguese style

When baking in the oven, always butter the sides of the mould, tray or casserole dish used. This prevents the sauce from sticking to the sides during cooking and makes the dish easier to clean afterwards.

What you need:
1.5 kg / 3 ½ lb cleaned hake, cut into 6 serving portions
125g / 4 oz butter, melted
125 ml / ½ glass dry white wine
250 ml / 1 cup breadcrumbs
125g / 6-8 med. close cob mushrooms, thinly sliced
45 ml / 3 tablespoons chives, finely chopped
2 tomatoes, peeled and sliced
6 anchovy fillets
30 ml / 2 tablespoons green pepper, finely chopped
1 large onion, thinly sliced
A good dash of olive oil
A pinch of grated nutmeg
A pinch of chilli pepper
A pinch of salt and pepper

How to make it:
1. Wash and almost dry the fish on absorbent paper and sprinkle with the salt, pepper, chilli and nutmeg.
2. Place the oil, onion and peppers in an ovenproof dish. Arrange the fish side by side on top. Place one anchovy fillet on each slice.
3. Place a slice of tomato on top of each anchovy. Sprinkle with the chives then top with the mushroom slices.
4. Drizzle the wine over the dish, cover with aluminium foil and place in the pre-heated oven for 25-30 minutes.
5. Now, remove the fish from the oven. Mix the breadcrumbs and the melted butter together and sprinkle over the fish. Continue baking uncovered in the oven for a further 5-10 minutes. Serve immediately with boiled rice.

Fisherman's delight
Stuffed baked runner trout

Runner trout or Mahie has become very popular among both chefs and restaurant goers all over the world because of its versatility. You can poach it, grill it, have it barbequed, pan fried or oven baked. The following recipe which comes from the Mazanderan region in Persia is popular pan fried and eaten with "Sabzei polo ba Mahie" (herbal rice.) It is also popular amongst the fishermen who live by the sea when it is stuffed and baked in the oven.

Serves 4-6

What you need:

1.8 kg / 4 lb Mahie, washed and scaled and patted dry with
   absorbent paper
One cup of water
60 g / 4 tablespoons butter, melted
60 g / 4 tablespoons or juice of one large lemon
2 medium tomatoes, sliced
2 medium onions, sliced
30 g / 2 tablespoons parsley, finely chopped
6 lemon wedges

For stuffing:

100g / ½ cup long grain or basmati rice, cooked in boiling salted water
   until tender and then drained
60 g / 4 tablespoons butter
1 onion finely chopped
1 celery stick, sliced
6 mushrooms, sliced
5 ml / 1 teaspoon grated lemon rind
A good pinch of salt and pepper to taste

How to make it:

1. Make the stuffing as follows:-Melt the butter in a pan. Add the onion, mushrooms and celery and sauté until the onion is transparent. Mix in the remainder of the ingredients.
2. Pack the stuffing into the fish cavity and close by sewing up with thread (preferably coloured).
3. Place the fish in a large greased baking dish with a little water. Brush the fish with the melted butter and pour the lemon juice over.
4. Bake in a pre heated oven for 20 minutes.
5. Arrange the tomato and onion slices alternatively on top of the fish.
6. Cover and bake for a further 20 minutes.
7. Serve with the parsley sprinkled over the top and place the lemon wedges on either side.

Alikreukel on fire

These giant sea snails are also known as large periwinkles or "olly crock" and are a much loved South African seafood.

Cleaning procedure:
1. They can be plucked from the rocks by hand and are washed and cleaned like mussels.
2. The cooking procedure is exactly like any shellfish such as mussels (see recipe page 29), but remove the snails with tongs from the boiling water. Shake the shell hard and the flesh should drop out.
3. Separate the meat, which remains attached to the snail's trapdoor, by using a sharp knife. The vicera should be cut away and discarded unless you want to cook your Alikreukel on fire.

How to cook on fire:
1. Allow the coals on the braai or B.B.Q. to die down to a medium heat.
2. Place the grid over at the point where it is hot.
3. Arrange the snails on the braai or B.B.Q. with their trapdoors facing upwards.
4. Allow the snails to stew in their own juices for 20 minutes.
5. The flesh can be lifted from the shells easily (discard the vicera by cutting it away).
6. Slice the flesh and serve with lemon garlic butter.

Spanish octopus

When looking at cuttlefish, squid and octopus one often thinks that there is no room or place for them on a dinner table. It may be surprising to know that these fish belong to the oyster, alikreukel and the famous escargot family. Oddly enough South Africans, Italians and Greeks have developed a taste for it. Octopus is the least versatile as it tends to be tough. It is however very tasty. Unless you are experienced in cleaning octopus you may find it a very messy business and so may prefer to ask your fishmonger to clean and prepare it for you. These days however octopus can usually be bought ready cleaned and prepared.

What you need:
900 g / 2 lb octopus, cleaned, cooked in their own juices for
   45 minutes and cut into chunks
60 ml / ⅓ rd cup olive oil
2 medium onions, sliced
450 g / 1 lb potatoes thinly sliced
1 clove garlic, crushed
½ glass sherry
2 bay leaves
A good pinch of chopped parsley
A pinch of turmeric
A pinch of salt and pepper

How to make it:
1. Panfry the onions with olive oil until golden.
2. Add the sherry, bay leaves and potatoes. Cover with the lid and simmer for 15 minutes.
3. Add crushed garlic, parsley and octopus.
4. Add the turmeric and season with salt and pepper.
5. Cover with the lid and simmer for a further 15 minutes.
6. Serve immediately.

Greek stuffed squid

This is a well established Greek dish, which is often served cold, for Summer buffets. It is however also delicious when it is eaten hot with crusty garlic bread. In the supermarkets and from the fishmongers squids are available and are usually about 10-15 cm long. Ask your fishmonger for the large squid tubes which are white and not greyish in colour.

Serves 4

4 (10-15 cm) squid. Cut the fins, tentacles and arms off. (see squid and preparing squid for cooking page 19)

For the stuffing:

45 ml / 3 tablespoons olive oil
250 g / 1 cup rice, cooked
30 ml / 2 tablespoons pine nuts
30 ml / 2 tablespoons currants
2 medium sized onions, chopped finely
30 ml / 2 tablespoons freshly chopped parsley

For the sauce:

60 ml / 4 tablespoons olive oil
60 ml / 4 tablespoons dry white wine
4 ripe tomatoes
45 ml / 3 tablespoons tomato paste
A good pinch of freshly chopped parsley
A pinch of crushed black pepper
A pinch of salt and pepper
125 g / ½ cup browned breadcrumbs

How to make it:

1. Soak the currants in water or wine overnight to become plump and juicy.
2. Fry the onions in a deep frying pan with a little oil until transparent.
3. Add the squid and the remaining ingredients for the stuffing one after the other and sauté, then set aside and cool.
4. Once cooled, stuff the squid, making sure not to over fill.
5. Sew the ends of the squid together with coloured thread.
6. Arrange the squid in a baking dish and set aside.
7. To make the sauce, simply mix all the ingredients with a little water and, pour over the squid, sprinkling the breadcrumbs and the chopped parsley on top.
8. Place the tray in a pre- heated oven for 30 minutes.
9. Remove, and serve immediately.

Perlemoen Provenąale
The mother of pearls

Perlemoen or abalone, is well known in Britain as a delicacy. It is the iridescent mother of pearls and is also known as Klipkous.

Serves 6

What you need:
6 perlemoen steaks
30 g / 2 tablespoons butter
15 ml / 1 tablespoon olive oil
2 medium onions, finely sliced
3 cloves of garlic, finely chopped
5 medium sized tomatoes, chopped
125 ml / ½ glass dry white wine
Pinch of sugar
A pinch of salt and pepper
2 bay leaves
Pinch of crushed black peppercorn

How to make it:
1. Sauté the perlemoen steaks with the butter and oil for 2-3 minutes in a frying pan.
2. Add the onion to the frying pan and sauté for a further 2-3 minutes.
3. Add the garlic, tomatoes, bay leaves, and wine. Season with the sugar, salt and pepper.
4. Cover with the lid, and simmer on a low heat for 1½ hours increasing the liquid by adding some wine or water to the pan if needed.
5. Serve with rice, pasta or sauté potatoes.

Moules marinière

This is probably the most popular dish in France. It is served mainly as a starter but makes a good main course as it is both nourishing and filling. For interesting variations try moules marinière with a little cream and fresh basil or caraway seeds plumped up in warm water.

Serves 4 or 2 greedy people

What you need:
48 fresh mussels, cleaned with beards removed (see page 18)
1 medium sized onion, finely chopped
60 ml / 4 tablespoons dry white wine
45 g / 3 tablespoons butter
A pinch of flour
A pinch of freshly chopped parsley

How to make it:
1. Place a knob of butter, onion, mussels and white wine in a saucepan. Cover the pan with a lid and place on a high heat, shaking occasionally from side to side and cooking for 4-5 minutes until the mussels have opened. Discard the ones that have not opened.
2. Arrange the mussels in 4 heated soup plates.
3. Blend the rest of the butter and flour into a smooth paste and add to the stock little by little.
4. Stir the sauce until it has thickened, pour over the mussels and sprinkle with the parsley. Serve with crusty garlic bread.

Prawns kiev

This dish can be served as a starter. Alternatively it could become your 'piece de resistance' as it makes a wonderful main course dish if two kievs are served on a bed of glazed spinach. Although the preparation takes a bit of time the results will win a round of applause. You can prepare this dish hours before serving and then fry the kievs when you are ready.

Serves 2

What you need:
8 king prawns, shelled and head and tailed
100 g / 6 tablespoons or 4 knobs of butter
2 eggs, beaten
1 clove garlic crushed
5 ml / 1 teaspoon French mustard
Some white dried breadcrumbs
Some flour
15 ml / 1 tablespoon freshly chopped parsley
A pinch of crushed black peppercorn
Enough oil for deep frying
A pinch of salt and pepper

How to make it:
1. Mix the parsley, salt, pepper, mustard, garlic and butter together.
2. Shape the butter mixture into 4 logs and place in greaseproof paper and refrigerate.
3. Cut open the belly of the prawns half way to make a butter fly shape with a sharp knife, being careful not to cut them in half.
4. Place two adjacent prawns between cling film and pound them with wet hands.
5. Mould the prawns round each log and roll lightly in the flour, eggs then in breadcrumbs. Dip again in the eggs and breadcrumbs to give a firmer coating and refrigerate until needed.
6. Deep fry, in hot oil for 3 minutes until golden brown. Drain and serve with salad leaves as a starter or with glazed spinach and vegetables as a main course.

Norwegian fish loaf

This dish can be cooked in the oven or on top of the stove. Its secret is to use a hand whisk to incorporate as much air as possible to ensure the loaf has a light fluffy texture.

Serves 4

What you need:
900 g / 2 lb white fish, skinned and boned
A good knob of butter
Enough bread crumbs, preferably white
30 ml / 2 tablespoons cornflour
250 ml / 1 cup milk
250 ml / 1 cup cream
A good pinch of salt and pepper

How to make it:
1. You need a loaf tin (mould) or casserole, buttered and dusted with breadcrumbs.
2. Sprinkle the fish with salt and pepper. Cut into pieces and blend in a food processor, a little at a time then tip the mixture into a large bowl and mix in the cornflour.
3. Mix the milk and cream together and add to the bowl, stirring into the mixture until it is light and fluffy. Pour into the mould and smooth the surface.
4. Place the cover on the mould or alternatively cover the dish with buttered foil or greaseproof paper. (Ensure that the cover is tightly fitting.)
8. To cook on top of the stove place the mould in a pan two thirds full of simmering water. If baking in the oven, stand the mould in a shallow tray of water.
6. Steam for one hour. Test the loaf to see if it is cooked by placing a knife in the pudding. If it comes out clean, turn out onto a hot serving dish.
7. This dish is normally served with a lemon butter sauce (see recipe on page 53).

Crayfish Thermidor

Crayfish tails are readily available from your fishmonger or fish market, cooked and prepared, live or frozen. Crayfish is also known as rock lobster and lives in the sea under rocky ledges. Make sure, the Crayfish is not over cooked (5 minutes for every 450g / 1 lb.)

Serves 2

What you need:
2 (450g / 1 lb) live Crayfish or just the tail
300 ml / 1¼ cups béchamel sauce (see recipe page 44)
45 g / 3 tablespoons butter
45 ml / 3 tablespoons olive oil
½ onion finely chopped
30 ml / 2 tablespoons cream
170 ml / 1 glass dry white wine
30 g / 2 tablespoons dried Parmesan cheese
5 ml / 1 teaspoon dried tarragon
5 ml / 1 teaspoon chopped parsley
5 ml / 1 teaspoon French mustard
250 g / 1 cup breadcrumbs
30 g / 2 tablespoons melted butter
Pinch of salt and pepper

How to make it:

1. To prepare the Cray fish see cleaning lobster instructions page 18.
2. Heat the oil and a knob (30g / 2 tablespoons) of butter together. Place the Crayfish cut side down in the frying pan and cover with a lid and cook for 14 minutes until the shell is red, turning once after 7 minutes.

3. Place the rest of the butter and the onion in a saucepan and fry for less than a minute. Add the wine and herbs and cook vigorously to reduce the sauce then add the béchamel and simmer over a low heat.
4. Remove the lobsters from the pan and strain the juice into the sauce. Add the cream and simmer for a further 2-3 minutes.
5. Remove the pan from the heat and add the mustard and half of the cheese and season to taste.
6. Remove the lobster meat from the shells and slice neatly. Remove the meat from the claws and chop coarsely.
7. Add 2 tablespoons of sauce to the claw meat and place in the head shell.
8. Place 1 tablespoon of sauce in the tail shells and replace the meat pieces into the shells.
9. Place the shells on a baking tray and coat with the rest of the sauce. Sprinkle with the breadcrumbs, the remaining cheese and a little melted butter.
10. Place in pre heated oven 400°C / 200°F for 10 minutes to brown.

Fillets of sole caprice

Although it is quite easy to skin and fillet a sole most fishmongers these days are happy to prepare it for you.

Serves 4

What you need:
8 fillets of sole, skinned
45 g / 3 tablespoons butter
15 ml / 1 tablespoon olive oil
2 bananas sliced lengthways and halved
2 eggs, well beaten
Juice of 1 lemon
45 ml / 3 tablespoons flour
105 ml / 7 tablespoons breadcrumbs
Pinch of salt and pepper
Pinch of freshly chopped parsley
Half a lemon, sliced

How to make it:
1. Season the fillets with the lemon juice, salt and pepper.
2. Place the fillets in the flour, then dip in beaten egg followed by the breadcrumbs, to coat evenly.
3. Heat the butter and oil in a frying pan. Fry the fillets, two at a time, until golden on both sides. Remove and place on absorbent paper.
4. Place the banana quarters in the frying pan with the remainder of the lemon juice and butter mixture and cook until soft but not broken.
5. Arrange two sole on each heated plate and top each fish with half a banana.
6. Garnish each fillet with a slice of lemon and sprinkle with parsley. Serve immediately.

Sea bream Véronique

This is a delightful summer dish in which seedless grapes are used to enhance the sauce. (Alternatively pips can be removed from seeded grapes.) The skins can be left on as they add an interesting flavour.

Serves 4

What you need:
1 kg / 2.2 lb sea bream, filleted
250g / 8 oz small green seedless grapes
30 g / 2 tablespoons butter, softened
250 ml / 1 cup cream
250 ml / 1 cup dry white wine
15 ml / 1 tablespoon flour
4 spring onions, finely chopped
Pinch of salt and pepper
Pinch of crushed black peppercorn

How to make it:
1. Place the spring onion in a buttered ovenproof dish and arrange the fish on top. Pour the wine over, season and place in a preheated oven for 15-20 minutes.
2. Place the cooked fish on a serving dish and keep warm.
3. Strain the liquid from the oven dish into a saucepan and bring to the boil. Add the cream, reduce, then add the grapes.
4. Melt the butter in another saucepan and stir in the flour for a few minutes. Add the sauce from the saucepan, season and pour over the fish.
5. Garnish with a few grapes and serve with vegetables.

Skate with orange and caper sauce

Skate with its great flavour does not need to have a sauce with lots of ingredients to enhance it. Just a simple sauce will do.

Serves 4

What you need:
900g / 2 lb skate wings, washed and divided into 4 portions
2 spring onions, washed and finely chopped
A knob of butter
Juice of 2 oranges
15 ml / 1 tablespoon capers
15 ml / 1 tablespoon freshly chopped parsley
Salt and pepper for seasoning
1.1 litres / 2 pints court bouillon, see recipe page 38

How to make it:
1. Place the skate in a shallow flameproof dish. Pour the court bouillon over it. Bring to the boil and poach gently for 20 minutes.
2. Melt the butter in a small saucepan and sauté the spring onion.
3. Stir in the orange juice and add the capers and chopped parsley. Season well.
4. Remove the skate from the court bouillon and scrape off the gelatinous skin from both sides with a knife. Place the skate in a serving dish and pour the sauce over it.

Baked trout enveloped
with almond and lime

Trout wrapped in protective silver foil with a little butter and wine added, cooks gently and evenly in a few minutes. All you have to do before baking, is to make sure that there are no holes in the foil or the juices will leak out. Trout flesh is so delicious and full of flavour that grilling tends to dry the flesh and rather spoil it. Most restaurants prefer to grill or oven bake trout without covering the fish with foil and it becomes crunchy and dry instead of being moist and firm.

Serves 4

4 medium sized trout, gutted, scraped and washed clean under
   running cold water
90 g / 4 oz butter
300 ml / ½ pint dry white wine
1 lemon, sliced
1 lime cut into wedges
50 g / 2 oz dried flaked almonds
4 bay leaves
A pinch of freshly chopped parsley
Salt and crushed black pepper for seasoning
Aluminium foil for wrapping

1. Grease the aluminium foil which must be at least 15 cm. (6 inches) longer and wider than your oven dish with a little knob of butter.
2. Place the foil inside the oven dish and put the remaining butter in the centre of the foil.
3. Place a couple of the lemon slices with one bay leaf inside the belly of the trout and season well.
4. Place the fish inside the foil and bring the sides up to make an open envelope.
5. Pour the wine into the envelope and sprinkle the fish with the almonds. Place the lime wedges on each corner and close the foil together tightly by turning the edges.
6. Put the dish in the pre-heated oven for 20-25 minutes.
7. Place the foil on a serving dish and open. Sprinkle the trout with parsley and serve.

Stuffed red mullet with Ricotta and spinach

This dish is as tasty as it is beautiful. The cooking method is exactly the same as for trout and that is how I keep the flesh moist and the flavour intact.

Serves 4

What you need:
4 (225-280 g) / (8-10 oz) red mullet, gutted with gills removed, scaled and fins cut off
225 g / 8 oz fresh spinach, stalks snapped off, washed with cold water, drained and cooked in a saucepan without water for a minute or two then squeezed dry
120 g / 4 oz ricotta cheese, finely diced
60 g / 2 oz butter
A pinch of freshly grated nutmeg
A pinch of thyme
A pinch of salt and pepper

How to make it:
1. Sauté the ricotta cheese with a little butter in a frying pan for one minute. Add the spinach and fry for a further minute on a low heat.
2. Add the nutmeg and the thyme and season well.
3. Fill the cavities of the fish with the stuffing.
4. Grease four pieces of aluminium foil. Place a little butter on each piece of foil and place the fish on top of each butter knob. Close the foil tightly.
5. Lay the foil envelopes next to each other in a large oven dish and place in a pre-heated oven for 20 minutes.
6. Remove the foil envelopes from the oven and transfer to serving plates. Open each envelope and serve immediately with brown rice or roasted potatoes.

Stuffed plaice, "not" the poor man's food

I find that stuffed fillets of plaice have a tendency to open up and come unrolled when being cooked. This problem can be solved by placing the rolls for half an hour or so in the fridge before cooking. When stuffing flat fish such as plaice or sole I like to use hazelnut and raisin with a little lemon juice as this goes very well with these fish.

Serves 6

What you need:
12 fillets of plaice or sole
50 g / 2 oz butter
1 medium sized onion, finely diced
125 g / 4 oz hazelnuts and raisins ground together
1 bowl of flour seasoned with salt and pepper
1 bowl of breadcrumbs, wholemeal
4 eggs, beaten
A good pinch of chopped parsley
Juice of 1 fresh lemon
Oil for frying

How to make it:
1. Fry the onion, hazelnuts and raisins in a frying pan with the butter. Cook over a low heat for 5-10 minutes. Add the parsley and one tablespoon of the breadcrumbs. Mix well and allow to cool.
2. Place the fish fillets on a board and divide the stuffing evenly between them. Roll up.
3. Dip each roll in flour, then egg and then the breadcrumbs.
4. Heat some oil in a frying pan, place the fish rolls in the pan and fry evenly.
5. Pour the lemon juice over the fish and serve.

Lobster with devil sauce

Don't be put off by this name even though your eyebrows may rise as you read and you may think why do I have to go to all this trouble. For most of us lobster is expensive, to others it is a real luxury. I prefer to eat lobster plainly cooked and find this sauce lifts the flavour without overwhelming it. Ask your fishmonger for a cooked lobster. Prepare it in advance and serve it cold with a salad and plenty of French dressing.

Serves 4

What you need:
2 x 450 g / 2 lb cooked lobsters, split and keep the claws for decoration
15 ml / 1 tablespoon tarragon vinegar
15 ml / 1 tablespoon creamed horseradish
60-75 ml / 4-5 tablespoons olive oil
15 ml / 1 tablespoon Worcestershire sauce or Tabasco
Juice of 1 lemon
A bunch of watercress
A pinch of salt and black pepper

How to make it:
1. Extract the lobster meat from the shell.
2. Place shells in centre of serving plates and fill with lobster meat.
3. Make the sauce by mixing the remaining ingredients together.
4. Pour the sauce over the meat and serve with salad.

Monkfish tagliatelli with sweet pepper sauce

Monkfish, due to its firm flesh, is an excellent fish for making sauce because it doesn't fall to pieces when it is stir-fried and goes very well with pasta dishes.

Serves 4

What you need:
450g / 1lb fresh or dried tagliatelli
335g / 12 oz monkfish fillet
1 medium onion, finely chopped
2 small red and green peppers, de-seeded and finely diced
1 clove garlic, crushed
1 celery stalk, finely sliced
30 ml / 2 tablespoons olive oil
1 glass white wine
1 glass single cream
2 tablespoons chopped parsley
seasoning (salt & pepper)

How to make it:
1. Boil the water in a saucepan. Place the pasta in for 4-5 minutes until al dente and set aside.
2. Heat the oil in a frying pan together with onion, garlic, peppers and celery. Fry gently for 5 minutes.
3. Remove the central bone from the monkfish and dice the flesh into 2cm (3/4") pieces and add to the saucepan, stir for a minute.
4. Add the white wine, stir and season. Cook for a further 3-4 minutes.
5. Stir in the cream and add the chopped parsley.
6. Serve immediately over the pasta.

Smoked haddock and spinach onion roulade

335g / 12oz smoked haddock
1 small onion, quartered
knob of butter
15 ml / 1 tablespoon olive oil
450g / 1lb fresh or 225g / 8oz frozen spinach, defrosted and strained to
   get rid of the excess water
2-3 bay leaves
6 eggs
1-2 dashes double cream
1-2 tablespoons grated Parmesan cheese
1 fist flour
1-2 glasses of milk
pinch of crushed peppercorn
pinch of salt & pepper

1. Place the washed spinach (if fresh) in an average saucepan without
   adding any liquid or water. Stir for 5 minutes, remove all liquid
   and set aside. Skin the haddock, place in a saucepan with the milk,
   bay leaves, onion and black peppercorn.
2. Boil two eggs until hard boiled. Peel and set aside.
3. Separate the rest of the eggs into two separate bowls.
4. Remove the haddock and strain the milk into a jug. Purée the fish
   in a food processor or mash it well and place in the yolk bowl. Mix
   well with cream and cheese.
5. Whip the egg whites until stiff and add to the fish mixture.
6. Lay a silver foil or a greaseproof paper (greased) on a Swiss roll
   tin or a baking sheet 33 x 23cm (13 x 9 inch).
7. Pour the soufflé mixture on and bake for 15 minutes, gas mark 6 /
   400°F / 200°C until golden.
8. Make a roux with the butter and flour in the flavoured milk to
   make a béchamel, stir until thick. Add the chopped hard boiled
   eggs and spinach and stir.
9. Remove the cooked soufflé mixture from the oven and turn it on to
   a clean tea towel on a work surface, pull off the paper or foil,
   spread with spinach mixture and roll up.
10. Slide onto a warm serving dish and serve immediately.

Turbot with ginger, tarragon and courgettes

This fish is expensive and restaurants charge the earth for it. If you cook it with care it is excellent in taste and texture. The preparation time isn't more than 5 minutes. The alternative way, if you want to use a whole trout without filleting it, is to add lime instead of lemon, courgettes to be julienne and pan fried separately instead of being grated, no ginger. Tarragon and hollandaise sauce is required. Just season and bake the fish uncovered with a dash of white wine, a little diced onion and two lime quarters in a preheated oven for 10-15 minutes.

Serves 4

What you need:
200 g / 4 x 7-8 oz turbot fillets, skinned and folded into 3 to make firm parcels and then placed on individual pieces of greased silver foil
2 courgettes, grated
15 ml / 1 tablespoon grated fresh ginger
45 ml / 3 tablespoons freshly chopped tarragon
30 ml / 2 tablespoons freshly squeezed lemon juice
15 ml / 1 tablespoon dry vermouth
500 ml / 2 cups hollandaise sauce (see recipe on page 40)
A pinch of coarse black pepper
Seasoning

How to make it:
1. Crown the fillet parcels with the grated courgettes, then sprinkle with the chopped tarragon and ginger.
2. Season with the coarse black pepper, seasoning and sprinkle with the lemon juice.
3. Fold the edges of the silver foil to make an envelope.
4. Place the parcels on a baking tray and then in a pre-heated oven to gas mark 5 / 375° F / 190°C for 20 minutes.
5. Beat the vermouth into the hollandaise sauce until a smooth texture has been reached.
6. Serve the sauce separately in a dish. Remove the parcels from the foil and place in the centre of the plate.

Halibut with mustard cream and leek julienne

I can't ever remember having served halibut with any other sauce than mustard cream. The reason is very simple. English mustard and turmeric blend very well together and the taste is absolutely divine.

Serves 2

What you need:

2 x 150-225 g / 6-8 oz halibut steaks, poached or pan fried for 1-2 minutes on each side
10 ml / 2 teaspoons English / Dijon mustard
½ a small onion, peeled and finely diced
225 g / 8 fl oz Béchamel (See page 44)
100 ml / 4 fl oz double cream
75 ml / 3 fl oz white wine
4 medium sized potatoes, peeled, boiled and mashed
1 medium sized carrot, peeled and grated
1 head of large leek, shredded lengthwise and fried into golden crisps
75 g / 3 oz butter
A pinch of crushed black peppercorn
A little salt and pepper

How to make it:

1. Place half of the butter in a frying pan. Add the onion and cook until golden.
2. Mix in the mustard.
3. Add the béchamel, two thirds of the cream and the white wine.
4. Add black peppercorn and seasoning. Reduce the sauce by half and set aside.
5. Place the mashed potato in a bowl and add the rest of the cream and the grated carrot. Mix well.
6. Place the potato in the centre of the serving plate.
7. Place the halibut on top of the mash and pour the sauce over it.
8. Pick a bundle of fried leeks and crown the halibut and serve.

Salmon dill with Icelandic prawns

I hardly know any one who does not like salmon. Salmon is cheap, full of texture and provides a healthy diet and above all it is one of my favourite fish when it comes to entertaining guests.

Serves 2

What you need:
2 x 215-250 g / 7-8 oz salmon fillets, skinned
100 g / 3 ½ oz Icelandic prawns
1 small onion, finely diced
1 knob of butter
60 ml / 2½ fl oz white wine
60 ml / 2½ fl oz fish stock (refer to page 37)
60 ml / 2½ fl oz whipping cream
30 ml / 2 tablespoons freshly chopped dill
A pinch of coarse black pepper
A little salt and pepper

How to make it:
1. Poach the salmon in boiling water or steam between two plates on top of a pan of boiling water until tender.
2. Heat the butter in a frying pan and add the onion cooking until golden.
3. Add the wine, prawns and the crushed black pepper and cook for one minute.
4. Add the fish stock, cream and seasoning.
5. Finally, add the chopped dill and simmer the sauce.
6. Place the salmon in the centre of the plate and pour the sauce over making sure the prawns sit on top of the salmon.

Brill with lemon sauce and fried julienne of smoked salmon

The fish is cooked whole and looks particularly good when brought to the table. Brill, with its moist texture, can be grilled and served with just butter, poached or even oven baked. Whichever way you decide to cook it, make sure this fish is off the bone. If you can't remove the bone yourself, ask your fishmonger to do this for you. What is important is to keep the fish in one piece, even if you decide to head and tail it.

Serves 2-3

670 g / 1 ½ lb whole Brill. Trim the fins and tail and de-bone, keeping the whole fish together
100g / 3 ½ oz butter
½ a small onion, finely diced
A pinch of flour
Grated rind and juice of one lemon
1 glass of dry white wine
250 ml / 1 cup fish stock (see page 37)
60 g / 2 oz smoked salmon, julienne
A pinch of crushed black peppercorn and a pinch of salt and pepper

1. Melt the butter in a frying pan, add the smoked salmon and fry until crisp. Set aside.
2. In the same frying pan, add onion and fry gently. Add the flour and mix to form a smooth texture.
3. Add the white wine and lemon juice and season with the black peppercorn, salt and pepper.
4. Add the fish stock and lemon rind and reduce by half.
5. Place the Brill in a piece of aluminium foil, shiny side in to keep the heat, and close tightly and then place on a baking tray.
6. Place the tray in a preheated oven gas mark 4 / 350°F / 180°C, for 20-25 minutes.
7. Remove the tray from the oven. Remove the foil and place the fish in the centre of an oval plate.
8. Pour the lemon sauce over the fish and arrange the smoked salmon on top and serve.

Escalope of shark with noisette butter, Capers and Anchovy

Shark escalope, capers and anchovy cream and parmentier potatoes, what are we celebrating? Obviously, it is not my birthday but this must be a treat!

Serves 2

4 x 125 g / 4 oz escallops of shark, thinly sliced
4 slices of fresh bread
6 fillets of anchovies
12 capers
225 g / 7-8 oz butter
30 ml / 2 tablespoons olive oil
15 ml / 1 tablespoon finely chopped fresh parsley
30 g / 1 oz plain flour
1 small onion finely diced
1 egg
Juice of ½ a lemon
250 ml / 1 cup milk
4 lemon wedges
A pinch of coarse black peppercorn

1. Put the bread into a food processor and convert into breadcrumbs.
2. Add the anchovies, capers, parsley and onion to the processor and blend, then place the mixture in a shallow dish.
3. Beat the egg into the milk and set aside. Mix the flour and crushed black pepper in another bowl and set aside.
4. Heat 50 g (2oz) of the butter and the oil in a frying pan.
5. Pass the escallops first through the flour, then the egg and milk mixture and finally coat with the breadcrumbs.
6. Now, fry the escallops until golden. Remove and transfer to a serving plate.
7. Heat the rest of the butter in a clean frying pan until it foams and smells nutty.
8. Add the lemon juice, pour over the escalopes and serve with lemon wedges.

John Dory fillets baked with
Almonds, Raisins and dry sherry

I find John Dory quite expensive for what it is. The taste, in my opinion, is similar to sole but some people may hold different views regarding this. Only one third of John Dory is edible so when preparing this fish you have to remember to take this into consideration if the fish isn't filleted.

Serves 6

What you need:
700g / 1.5 lb   John Dory fillets
150g / 6 oz butter
30 ml / 2 tablespoons olive oil
1 large onion, peeled and finely sliced
1 large glass of medium Sherry
A fist of almond flakes
A fist of dried raisins
A pinch of grated nutmeg
A pinch of salt and crushed black pepper

How to make it:
1. Heat only 2 oz (50g) of the butter with the oil in a frying pan.
2. Add the onion and cook until transparent.
3. Add the nutmeg, almonds, raisins, seasoning and the sherry and cook for a minute or two then pour into an ovenproof dish.
4. Put the John Dory fillets in the ovenproof dish and dot them with bits of the remaining butter. Cover with a lid or piece of aluminium foil.
5. Bake in a pre-heated oven 190°C / 375°F / gas mark 5 for 30 minutes.
6. Remove the foil and bake for a further 5 minutes before serving.

Curried coconut plaice with bananas

This way of cooking flat fish such as sole or plaice is very much an Indonesian or West Indian dish. The outcome is the splendid crispness of the fish which is served on a plate of hot fried bananas.

Serves 4

What you need:
4 plaice, skinned and filleted
60 ml / 4 tablespoons oil
2 eggs, beaten in a bowl
60 ml / 4 tablespoons coconut, shavings or desiccated
15 ml / 1 tablespoon mild curry powder
A pinch of salt and pepper
2 large bananas, peeled and cut length wise in half
1 lemon, cut into 4 wedges

How to make it:
1. In a bowl, mix the coconut, curry powder and seasoning together.
2. Take each fish fillet and dip in the egg, then in the coconut mixture.
3. Heat the oil in a frying pan and fry the fillet on both sides, turning only once.
4. Keep the fried fillets hot in an ovenproof dish in the oven.
5. In the same frying pan, fry the bananas on both sides, remove and place in the centre of the serving plate.
6. Place the fillets on top and serve with lemon wedges.

King prawn goulash

Goulash is a very good dish for the figure conscious because all it consists of is a thick stew of peppers, onions, tomatoes and a little water (or vegetable stock) which is reduced during cooking. Add whole mushrooms to the dish and it is called mushroom goulash. When fish is used such as in this recipe the goulash is named after the fish.

Serves 2

What you need:
12 medium size king prawns, peeled
1 knob of butter
15 ml / 1 tablespoon olive oil
½ a red pepper, thinly sliced
½ a green pepper, thinly sliced
1 large onion, roughly chopped
4 tomatoes, finely diced or 1 small tin of plum tomatoes mashed
  with a fork
One dash of cream
1 cup of natural yoghurt
1-2 cups of water or vegetable or even fish stock
A pinch of paprika
Salt and crushed black pepper to season

How to make it:
1. Heat the oil and butter in a saucepan. Fry the onions, peppers and prawns for a few minutes until the vegetables soften.
2. Add the tomatoes, stock, yoghurt and simmer to reduce.
3. Add the cream, paprika and seasoning and cook for further minute.
4. Serve immediately with rice.

Bacon wrapped roasted monkfish and Tomato Aioli

This is a perfect fish for stir frying and grilling. However when you wrap monkfish up with bacon, it becomes something to die for! Bacon keeps the flesh moist and whilst it is cooking these two complement each other with their flavours in a way that I could only describe as perfect.

Serves 6

What you need:
1.4 kg / 3 lb monkfish tail
4 fresh tomatoes finely diced
1 small onion, finely diced
1-2 cloves of garlic, crushed
30 ml / 2 tablespoons olive oil
Pinch of dried thyme
6-8 thinly cut rashers of streaky bacon
Pinch of salt and pepper for seasoning

How to make it:
1. Cut off the membrane of the monkfish from the outside after being trimmed.
2. Cut off the flesh of the monkfish from the back bone.
3. Keep the 'cut offs' for making the fish stock.
4. Wrap the fillet of monkfish in bacon rashers and place in the roasting tin. Cook in a little stock in a pre-heated oven, 190°C / 375°F / gas mark 5, for up to half an hour.
5. Meanwhile, heat the oil in a frying pan and cook the onion and garlic until it changes colour.
6. Add the tomatoes, thyme and seasoning (and a little water if needed) and simmer for 2 minutes.
7. Divide and pour the sauce equally onto the centres of the six serving plates.
8. Remove the monkfish from the oven and slice into six. Place each portion in the centre of the tomato sauce before serving.

Tuna with black butter sauce

The secret of many good fish recipes lies in contrasting the fish with a slightly sharp sauce. Just add a little malt vinegar to your fish and chips, a little lemon juice to your Sea bass, or black butter sauce which is sharpened with white wine vinegar and capers to complement your Tuna.

Serves 4

What you need:
225 g / 4 x 8 oz tuna steaks
2 –3 cups of court bouillon, see page 38
30 g / 1 oz capers
180 g / 6 oz salted butter
30 ml / 2 tablespoons red wine vinegar
15 g / ½ oz freshly chopped parsley

How to make it:
1. Place the tuna in a shallow frying pan with the court bouillon and bring to the boil and simmer for 15 minutes. Drain and keep the tuna warm in a serving dish.
2. Sprinkle the tuna with the capers.
3. Heat the butter in a frying pan until it foams, begins to go dark and smells nutty.
4. Pour the vinegar into the frying pan, then add the parsley.
5. After 30 seconds, pour over the tuna and serve.

King prawns with garlic and lemon herb butter

This fish is amazingly popular with restaurant goers in Britain. This fish is so delicious, especially when it is cooked in garlic lemon herb butter that you don't even have to be hungry to eat it.

Serves 2

What you need:
16 jumbo king prawns, head, tailed, shelled and butterflied
90 g / 3 oz butter
5 ml / 1 teaspoon olive oil
Juice of ½ a lemon
2-3 cloves of garlic, finely crushed
15 ml / 1 tablespoon of parsley, freshly chopped
A pinch of crushed black peppercorns
Salt and pepper to season

How to make it:
1. Place the garlic in a frying pan with the butter and oil on a high heat.
2. Shallow fry the king prawns with the garlic butter on both sides until the colour changes.
3. Add the parsley and lemon juice.
4. Add the black peppercorn and seasoning and serve immediately with a salad.

Angels on horseback

This is a fish dish that you can prepare partially in advance. The angel fish can be grilled and kept in a cool oven before serving. The horses need to be cooked when you are ready to eat.

Serves 6

Order of work:
1. 12 oysters, wrapped in 12 streaky bacon rashers
2. Grill the angels and keep in a cool oven
3. Grill the oysters, until the bacon is crisp
4. Remove the crusts from 6 slices of sliced bread. Toast then cover with butter
5. Place the toast in the centre of the plate
6. Crown with the angel fish
7. Top with the oysters and serve

Prawn patia

This is a dish which is as spicy as a curry dish even though it is made without curry powder. It is extremely popular amongst American Indians and is very much considered a classic "Parsee" dish.

Serves 4

36 king or large North Atlantic Prawns, unshelled
300 ml / ½ pint of fish stock
Enough olive oil
2 large onions, finely diced
1 clove garlic crushed
4 green chillies, finely chopped
4 red chillies, finely chopped
Juice of one lemon
15 ml / 1 tablespoon turmeric powder
A handful of fresh coriander finely chopped
30 ml / 2 tablespoons vinegar
15 ml / 1 tablespoon brown sugar
5 ml / 1 teaspoon cumin seeds
1 green mango finely diced (optional)
A pinch of crushed black peppercorn
A pinch of salt and pepper

1. Blend the garlic, chillies and coriander leaf to a paste with some salt and one tablespoon of vinegar.
2. Add and mix the cumin and crushed black peppercorn.
3. Fry the paste in oil for a few minutes, add the turmeric and sugar and stir well.
4. Add the lemon juice, remaining tablespoon of vinegar and the mango and stir again.
5. Fry the onion in a separate pan and add it to our sauce with half of the fish stock.
6. Simmer until the mixture begins to dry out, then add the remaining stock and the prawns.
7. Cook for 5 or more minutes to achieve a sticky consistency and serve.

Hake au Poivre with red pepper relish

This dish, as unusual as it sounds, is a classic version of steak au poivre. Alternative choices to hake could be monkfish, cod or haddock.

Serves 4

What you need:
4 x 175g / 6 oz Hake steaks
45 ml / 3 tablespoons olive oil
15 ml / 1 tablespoon balsamic vinegar
45 ml / 3 tablespoons mixed peppercorns
2 small red peppers, seeded, cut lengthways and finely diced
4 Anchovy fillets (out of tin), chopped
12 capers
4 ripe tomatoes, peeled, seeded and quartered
2 cloves of garlic, finely crushed
16 Basil leaves, - 8 finely shredded and 8 for garnishing
A pinch of salt and pepper

How to make it:
1. Crush the peppercorns coarsely with a pestle and cover the fish with it. Sprinkle the salt and pepper over the fish.
2. Heat a little of the olive oil and fry the peppers for a few minutes until tender. Add the garlic, tomatoes, anchovies and 8 shredded basil leaves and stir, simmering until soft.
3. Stir the capers and balsamic vinegar into the contents of the pan, season and keep hot.
4. In a frying pan heat the olive oil and fry the fish on both sides, turning them only once.
5. Transfer the fish to individual serving plates and place the relish next to the fish. Garnish with the remaining basil leaves and serve.

Red mullet Saltimbocca

This dish again is another classic version to that of Saltimbocca which is normally made with veal. By rubbing some saffron into the skin, the rich colour of red mullet is intensified and makes this a perfect complement to the Parma ham.

Serves 4

What you need:
8 Red mullet, fillets, scaled (not skinned)
8 Parma ham slices, thinly cut
8 fresh sage leaves
15-30 ml / 1-2 tablespoons olive oil
115g / 4 oz mixed olives
A knob / 25g or 2 tablespoons butter
A pinch of saffron threads or powder
A pinch of salt and pepper

For the dressing:
300 ml / ½ pint extra virgin olive oil.
105 ml / 7 tablespoons balsamic vinegar.
15 ml / 1 tablespoon caster sugar.
1 small courgette, finely diced.
1 small red pepper, finely diced.
1 ripe tomato, peeled, seeded and finely diced.

How to make it:
1. Score the red mullet lightly in 3-4 places, rub the saffron with a little olive oil on both sides of the fillets.
2. In a frying pan, starting with the skin side down fry the fillets (in the remaining oil) on each side for not more than 2 minutes along with the olives and seasoning. Remove and dry on absorbent paper.
3. Place a sage leaf on top of each fillet and wrap with a slice of Parma ham. Fry again in the butter for less than a minute on either side and transfer to a warm serving plate and keep hot.
4. To serve make the dressing, by mixing all the ingredients together, and drizzle it over and around the fish.

Green Fish Curry

This classic dish is one of my favourite curries. It is called green fish because of all the herbs used in making the sauce which gives the dish its rich colour. This is a delicious curry which compliments exotic fish such as Sword fish, Mahi, Hoki or Coley. When serving this dish make sure you accompany it with some sort of fragrant basmati rice and some lemon wedges.

Serves 4

What you need:
750 g. -1 Kg / 1½ -2 lbs Hoki fillets, skinned
150 ml / ¼ pint sunflower or ground nut oil
75 ml / 5 tablespoons sesame oil
45 ml / 3 tablespoons fish stock
400 ml / 14 fl oz coconut milk
15 ml / 1 tablespoon shrimp paste
6 spring onions chopped
2 small red onions, finely chopped
4 clove of garlic, roughly chopped
15 ml / 1 tablespoon fresh root ginger, peeled and roughly chopped
2 fresh green chillies, seeded and roughly chopped
Juice and grated rind of 1 lemon
A pinch of coriander seeds
A pinch of five spice powder
A hand full each of chopped fresh coriander, mint and basil
1 lemon, quartered
A pinch of salt and pepper
Fresh chillies and coriander to garnish

How to make it:
1. To make the curry paste, combine the root ginger, garlic, green chillies, lemon juice, coriander seeds, five spice powder and half of the sesame oil into a processor and whiz to a fine paste and set aside.
2. Pour the rest of the sesame oil into a large pan and fry the red onion for 2 minutes. Add the fish and stir fry for a further 2 minutes.
3. Lift out the fish and onion onto a plate and set aside.
4. Pour the paste mixture into the pan and add the shrimp paste and stir. Return the fish and onion to the pan.
5. Add the coconut milk and simmer for 5 minutes.
6. Meanwhile, process the herbs, spring onion, lemon rind and sunflower / groundnut oil in a processor and whiz to a coarse paste.
7. Stir this paste into the fish curry and add the fish stock. Garnish with fresh chillies and coriander and serve with fragrant rice and lemon wedges.

Trout with Tamarind and Thai sauce

Trout is cheap, delicious, full of flavour and very much available but in most restaurants chefs try to inspire the taste with some sort of spicy sauce to give it that little bit of extra zing it needs to transform it into an extra special dish.

Serves 4

For the Trout
4 x 350g / 12 oz trout, gutted and cleaned
1 knob of butter
8 spring onions, the heads being cut into diagonal slices
60 ml / 4 tablespoons soy sauce
30 ml / 2 tablespoons fresh coriander, chopped

For the Sauce
50g / 2 oz Tamarind pulp
45 ml / 3 tablespoons fish stock
Some boiling water
15 ml / 1 tablespoon olive oil
2 shallots, roughly chopped
1 fresh chilli pepper, seeded and chopped
8 ml / ½ tablespoon ginger freshly chopped
15 ml / 1 tablespoon brown sugar
A pinch of salt and pepper

1. Make a few light slashes on both sides of the trout and fill the cavity with the heads of the spring onions and half the chopped coriander.
2. Coat the trout with the soy sauce and place in an ovenproof dish. Sprinkle the remainder of the chopped spring onions and the coriander over the fish and set aside until required.
3. To make the sauce, place the tamarind in a small bowl, cover with boiling water and mash with the back of a spoon until soft, then pour into a blender along with the olive oil. Add the shallots, fresh chilli, ginger, sugar, fish stock and seasoning and whiz to a coarse texture.
4. Pour the sauce over the trout, place a knob of butter on top, season well and cook in the oven at 180°C / gas mark 4 / 350°F for 10-15 minutes. Serve immediately.

Bonito (Skip Jack)

This fish with its unique character is also known as Skip Jack but the closest fish that resembles it must be tuna. Bonito is a fish for every day use.

Serves 4

What you need:
900g / 2 lbs Bonito, cleaned and cut into 2 cm. (¾ inch) steaks
100 ml / 7 tablespoons olive oil
100 ml / 7 tablespoons chicken stock
450g / 1 lb onions, finely sliced
2 garlic cloves, finely chopped
2 sprigs of parsley
A drizzle of vinegar
1 teaspoon paprika
Some coarse salt
Some flour
Some strips of seared red pepper or canned pepper
A pinch of salt and pepper

How to make it:
1. Coat the fish in flour and season with some coarse salt.
2. Fry the fish in a frying pan of olive oil on both sides and lift and set aside.
3. In the same frying pan, fry the onion, garlic, parsley, paprika and vinegar for 2 minutes.
4. Add the stock to the sauce, season with salt and pepper and simmer to reduce.
5. Place the fish in the centre of the serving plates, pour the sauce over and decorate with strips of red pepper and serve.

Loup de mer Farci

In English the term 'Loup de mer' is known as Sea Bass and Farci, just means stuffed or filled. This is the way the French people like to eat sea bass - by stuffing it in order to keep all the flavours in.

Serves 2

What you need:
1½ kg / 3½ lb sea bass, scaled and gutted
60 ml / 4 tablespoons olive oil
30 ml / 2 tablespoons white wine vinegar
A dash of brandy
1 onion, thinly sliced
A pinch of fresh thyme, finely chopped or (dried)
2 tomatoes, finely sliced
60 ml / 4 tablespoons tomato sauce, freshly made
60 ml / 4 tablespoons tarragon mustard
A pinch of salt and pepper for seasoning

How to make it:
1. To fill the cavity of sea bass, use only some of the onion, tomato, thyme and tarragon mustard.
2. Make a few slanting cuts along the sides of the fish, rub the rest of the tarragon mustard in and season with the salt and pepper.
3. Insert a slice of the remaining tomato and onion into the cuts. Sprinkle with the olive oil and vinegar and a dash of brandy, also the remainder of the thyme over the fish before baking in the oven for about 20-25 minutes at gas mark 4 / 180°C / 350°F.
4. Remove the fish from the oven and transfer to the centre of your serving dish. Pour the juice over and serve.

Baked Stuffed Herrings

This fish is cheap and probably the most important food fish in the modern world. Herrings are mostly salted and smoked. Most Europeans like to eat them raw. In America young herrings are canned as sardines, and the larger ones are stuffed and eaten as a main dish.

Serves 4

What you need:
4 Herrings, medium - large size, cleaned and dried
Some drippings of olive oil
1 medium sized onion, minced finely
15-30 ml / 1-2 tablespoons fine breadcrumbs
7-8 ml / ½ tablespoon mixed herbs
A pinch of parsley, finely chopped
A little pinch of salt and pepper
A few drops of lemon juice

How to make it:
1. Cut off the heads and tails of the herrings.
2. Open them down the back and take out the back bones.
3. Mix the minced onion with the breadcrumbs.
4. Add the herbs and parsley with a little salt and pepper and mix well with a few drops of lemon juice.
5. Stuff the inside of the herring with the mixture and lay another herring over it, making a sort of sandwich.
6. Put the pairs of herrings on a greased baking tin and drizzle some olive oil over them.
7. Cover with foil and bake for about 20– 30 minutes in a preheated oven gas mark 4 / 180°C / 350°F
8. Baste occasionally. Remove from the oven and serve immediately.

Tuna with Spiced Herb Tomato

You are in a rush or maybe you have some unexpected guests coming for dinner and you don't want to spend so much time in the kitchen. This is the solution, prepare the sauce in advance, cool it down and refrigerate until dinner is to be served.

Serves 4

What you need:
4 x 200g / 7-8 oz tuna steak
30 ml / 2 tablespoons olive oil
1 clove of garlic, finely crushed
1 medium onion, finely diced
50-60g / 2-3 oz butter
4 large tomatoes, diced or 1 tin of chopped plum tomatoes
2-3 green chilli peppers, diced
1 glass of dry white wine
1 teaspoon dried thyme
1 teaspoon dried basil
pinch of salt & pepper

How to make it:
1. Divide the butter into 4 lumps and place on top of the tuna steak in a large oven dish.
2. Place the tuna in a preheated oven for not more than ten minutes.
3. Meanwhile, fry the onion, chillies and garlic until golden.
4. Add chopped tomatoes and a little water.
5. Add thyme and basil, season and reduce the sauce.
6. Add white wine and reduce the sauce.
7. In a serving dish, place the tuna on top of the creamed mash (4 pounded potatoes with a little butter) and drizzle the sauce around it.

Oven Baked Salmon with Chives and lemon in a white wine dressing

The order of the work:
1. De-scale the whole salmon
2. The salmon should then be gutted and rinsed under cold water.
3. Salmon should be headed and tailed and rinsed again under cold water.
4. Place the salmon in an oven dish.
5. Add a glass or two of dry white wine.
6. Sprinkle 2-3 tablespoons of finely diced onion.
7. Sprinkle 2-3 tablespoons of chopped chives.
8. Place 2 knobs of butter on top of the salmon.
9. Place 4 lemon quarters on top of the fish.
10. Season well and bake in a pre-heated oven for 15-20 minutes and serve.

Sea bass on String of Pasta

The order of work:
1. Bake the sea bass in an ovenproof dish covered with aluminium foil in a preheated oven with one medium finely chopped onion, a glass of dry white wine and a knob of butter for ten minutes.
2. Remove the foil, season well with salt and pepper and place back in the oven for a further 10 minutes.
3. Meanwhile, place enough spaghetti or tagliatelle pasta in salted boiling water for 2-3 minutes until the pasta is Al Dente.
4. Serve the pasta in the centre of the plate.
5. Remove the fish from the oven and place the sea bass on top.
6. Drizzle the leftover sauce in the oven dish on top of the sea bass and serve.

Red mullet with Cherry tomatoes in a sauce of capers and olives

This dish is as pleasant as the one which is stuffed with ricotta and spinach and as tasty. The cooking method for me is exactly the same as the one for the trout and that is how I keep the flesh moist and flavour intact.

Serves 2

What you need:
2 (225 – 280g / 8-10oz) red mullet, gutted and gills removed, scaled and fins cut off
4 Bay leaves
60g / 2oz butter
8-12 cherry tomatoes
8-12 green olives, pitted
8-12 capers
1 lemon, quartered
pinch of freshly grated nutmeg
pinch of thyme
pinch of salt & pepper

How to make it:
1. Wash the fish under cold water.
2. Add the nutmeg and the thyme and season well.
3. Fill the cavities of each fish with two bay leaves.
4. Providing you have a large oven dish, grease two pieces of aluminium foil. Put a little butter on each foil and place the fish on top of each butter knob. Throw a few olives, capers and a few cherry tomatoes on top, then close the foil tightly around the fish.
5. Put the foil next to each other in the oven dish and place in a preheated oven for 10 minutes.
6. Remove from the oven, open the foil and put two lemon quarters on top of each fish and cook uncovered like an open envelope for a further 5 minutes. Serve immediately.

A Connoisseur's Guide

Final words

People tend to think that the seafood of one sea or ocean is different to the seafood of others. Now that, the world has shrunk, it has become commonplace for fish to be flown from for example the Persian Gulf to Japan, South Africa to England, New Zealand to California or from South America to France in fact from almost anywhere in the world to anywhere.

I have tried to talk about the origins of the relevant fish in detail and I hope that you the reader will be satisfied with the general knowledge of the most commonly used fish as well as the recipes that I have included from Europe, especially those from Britain, and from the rest of the world.

As for the names, you must have noticed that I have given the relevant name from which country the recipe originated. For instance, Chinese names are given in their Cantonese form, which will be useful if you are going to visit China, be it on holiday or business or just visiting a Chinese or Cantonese restaurant. Many names are quite confusing and the types of fish beyond imagination. For instance, the common grey mullet has over forty different names in Italy and at the same time the Murray Cod of Australia is not even a sea fish. Therefore, the list of names in this last chapter should only be used as a general guide and not as a dictionary.

Fish is the name

English	French	German	Russian	Spanish	Chinese
Salmon	Saumon	Lachs	Nerka	Salmon	Sake
Sardines	Sardine	Sardine	Sardina	Sardina	Iwashi
Anchovies	Anchois	Sardelle	Anchous	Anchoa	Fung mei
Herrings	Hareng	Hering	Sel'd'		Nishbin
Eels	Anguille	Flussaal	Ugor'	Anguila	Sin
Cod	Cabillaud	Dorsch	Pertui	Bacalao	Tara
Hake	Merluche	Seehecht	Chek	Merluza	
Haddock	Eglefin	Schellfisch	Piksha	Eglefino	
Sea Bass	Loup de mer	Seebarsch		Lubina	
Sea Bream	Sar			Sargo	Ma yau
Red Mullet	Rouget	Meerbarbe		Salmonete	Hung sin
Blue Fish	Tassergal	Blaufisch	Lufar	Anjova	
Snappers	Vivaneau	Schnapper		Pargo	Hung yu
Mackerel	Auriou	Makrele	Skumbriya	Caballa	Faa gau
Tuna	Thon	Thunfisch	Tunets	Atun	Cam chaeng yu
Sword Fish	Espadon	Schwertfisch	Mech-ryba	Pez espada	Chien yu
John Dory	Gal	Peterfisch		Pez de San Pedro	Kanetat aki
Turbot	Turbot	Steinbutt	Tyurbo	Rodaballo	
Plaice	Carrelet	Scholle	Morskaya Kambala	Platija	
Sole	Sole	Seezunge	Morskoi yazyk	Lenguado	
Halibut	Fletan	Heilbutt			
Dog Fish	Emissole	Glatthai	Kun'ya	Musola	
Angel Shark	Ange de mer	Meerengel		Angelote	
Skate	Raie	Rochen	Skat	Raya	Saa po
Lobster	Homard	Hummer	Omar	Bogavante	
Shrimps	Crevette grise	Krabbe	Seraya krevetka	Quisquilla	Ha
Prawns	Crevette	Garnele	krevetka	Camaron	Gwai ha
Crab	Dormeur	Taschenkrebs	Oval' nyyikrab	Buey	

144

English	French	German	Russian	Spanish	Chinese
Cuttlefish	Seiche	Tintenfisch		Jibia	Mak mo
Squid	Encornet	Kalmar	Kal'mar	Calamar	Tor yau yu
Octopus	Pieuvre	Krake		Pulpo	Saa liu
Oysters	Huitre	Auster	Ustritsa	Ostra	Mau lai
Mussels	Moule	Miesmuschel	Midiya	Mejillon	Hoy meng phu
Scallops	Coquille Saint-Jacques	SchelpKamm-schel	Grebeshok	Concha de peregrino	Hung mao gan
Cockles	Bucarde	Herzmuschel	Berberecho		
Clams	Mye	Sandklaffmus-chel		Navaja	Chi kap law

Salmon:
Start life as a tiny **blob** in deep gravel when the parent fish deposit their eggs. As Salmon gain size they become known as **Parr,** and when they make their way out to the salt water of the sea they are called **Smolts.** Salmon after one year at sea are called **Grilse** but it is only after the age of 2 that adult fish become known as **Salmon.** Close relatives of salmon are: sea trout, salmon trout and brown trout—these are best poached.

Sardines:
Most people are confused about **Sardines** and **Pilchards.** The truth is that sardines are young pilchards or pilchards grow up to become sardines. French sardines are excellent when grilled, or beheaded, gutted, butterflied, boned and put in a pair together (skin side out) in batter and deep fried in the Algerian manner. Pilchards are best for making pies.

Anchovies:
The salty flavour of these fish make them great as flavouring agents. In earlier days they were eaten unsalted either fresh or frozen and not from the tin which is salted and popular. Although anchovies do not have special importance in Asian cookery they are very popular when it comes to European cuisine.

Herrings:
The common length of this fish is about 25 cm (7") and herrings have their own characteristics. The most important herrings are Atlantic herrings. There are several ways of curing herrings including: Hot smoking (English Bloater) which is ready to eat and does not keep long. Cold smoking (notably the Kipper) which needs to be cooked but keeps longer and pickling (rollmops) which people have the greatest demand for and which keep the longest.

Eels:
Some Eels have a very long life span and can live for 50 years. Eels are generally grey in colour but when they reach the age of sexual maturity they turn dark yellow. In autumn they undergo a further change and turn silver. Eel flesh is rich in fat and their coating makes them very slippery. Eels are good for soups and a variety of dishes including spit roasts.

Cod:
This is the most important fish in the history of mankind and can weight up to 90 kg (200 lb) and measures up to 2 metres (6'). The average weight in fish markets is only about 4 kg (9 lb). The colour of Cod varies and the lateral line can be pale grey, greenish or reddish depending on the fish's habitat. Cod feeds on other fish and its flesh which flakes easily is excellent. In Europe, especially in England, cod is very popular as fish and chips.

Hake:
This fish was originally referred to as being of the Cod family and could reach a length of 1 m (3'3"). If the hake's mouth is grey black inside, the fish is known as silver hake. Hake is mainly popular in Portugal and Spain where some think that it is the best fish of the cod family.

Haddock:
This fish belongs to the same family as cod. It can reach up to 80cm (32") long, but its normal length in fish markets is between 40-60cm (16"-24"). Haddock has a dark greenish brown or purplish grey back and is considered a close competitor to cod as far as English people and fish and chips are concerned. Haddock, as mentioned earlier can

be smoked and dried. Haddock roe is considered a delicacy but is less well known than cod roe.

Sea bass:
This is the most prized fish of Europe. A silvery fish with a maximum length of 1m (40"). The flesh is basically free of small bones and holds its shape after cooking. Sea bass can be poached, grilled or served cold and is mainly accompanied with a herbal flavoured butter sauce.

Sea bream:
Large or small, this is the fish for the fishmonger's display. Sea Bream comes from the family of Sparidae. For example, Bogue, Pandor, striped bream and saddle bream are all sea bream. Sea bream are best cooked grilled or baked in the oven. There are also red and black bream and these varieties can reach to a maximum length of 50 cm (21").

Red mullet:
This is among the most prized fish of the Mediterranean and is distinguished by their delicate flesh, red colour, and twin barbels which they use to frisk the bottom of the sea with for food. The smallest fish are about 25 cm (10") in length and the biggest 40 cm (16"). Red mullet are also known as Goat fish in Asian waters. There are over a dozen different varieties of red mullet in the Indian Pacific waters which range from East Africa and the Persian Gulf up to China and Japan, and down to Australia and New Zealand. In Mediterranean countries, people fry, bake or grill red mullet and in Asian countries they are often boiled or steamed.

Blue fish:
Almost every country thinks that this fish can only be found in their waters. In Persia in the Mazanderan Sea, in Turkey the beloved 'Lufer' as they call it, is to be found only in the region of the Bosphorus sea. Indians think that it is only found in the Indian Ocean whereas Romanians think it is only available from the Black Sea. Blue fish, may reach a length of 1.2 m (4') and swim in groups like a pack of hungry wolves destroying everything before them - it is no wonder they are called cannibals. These fish have a moderately oily flesh and

can be grilled, poached, baked or fried. In some countries you can even find smoked blue fish.

Snappers:
Snappers are mainly of a medium size and adult fish are typically about 35-60 cm (14"-25") long. They have a long pointed head and canine like teeth and jaws that can snap vigorously - hence the name. Snappers are outstandingly good to eat and the skin usually has red or yellow stripes which depict from which ocean they originate. Red snappers are best grilled or baked.

Mackerel:
This is a very handsome fish and is flashy in appearance. Mackerel can be recognised by their greeny-blue back markings and dark curving lines and white belly. The maximum length is 35 cm (14") and these fish are known as oceanic fish. Mackeral is a very oily fish and that is why sauces such as gooseberry, cranberry, rhubarb and sometimes tomato, go very well with it. Smoked mackerel, needs no further cooking and is good for making pâté.

Tuna:
The other name for tuna is tunny. This is an oceanic fish of medium to large size. The largest found in Atlantic and Pacific waters was 3 m (10') long and weighed about 679 k (2150 lb).   There are many different types of tuna the most well known being: blue fin tuna, big eye tuna, black fin tuna, yellow fin tuna and Skipjack tuna. The best part of the tuna to eat is its belly as the flesh is firm. Tuna normally appears on our dinner tables as steak and is good fried or grilled. Tinned tuna is also readily available and is used mainly for sandwiches and in salads.

Sword fish:
This fish is a big fish with a maximum length of 4 m (13') and is famous for its sword, which is not for making a hole in boats but for killing or stunning its prey. In cookery terms these fish are referred to as broad billed sword fish to distinguish them from **Marlin** and other similar species from the same family. Sword fish often laze on the surface of the water and this makes them easy to catch. The flesh of the fish is of a very compact structure and steaks can be grilled,

poached or married off with some kind of tomato sauce, or with lemon and olive oil.

John Dory:
This fish with its remarkable shape, can reach a length of 60 cm (2') and weighs as much as 3 kg (7 lb) but in fish markets you find that they are normally only half this size. The mouths of John Dory can open very wide with some of the bones being of striking shapes and it is for this reason that people in Turkey call them carpenter fish. The head and gut of the fish accounts for two thirds of its weight. Regardless of the waste John Dory makes an excellent fillet. In France the name for this fish is "poule de mer"

Turbot:
This fish and Dover sole, both of which are found in European waters, are two of the finest flat fish available. Turbot possibly scores slightly better than Dover sole as it is a bigger and meatier fish. The skin is normally greyish or sandy brown and is covered in tiny bony tubercles. Turbot, because of its firm flesh, is mainly cooked by steaming and is usually served with Mousseline sauce.

Plaice:
This fish is instantly recognizable with large red and orange spots on a brown back. Most popular in Europe, plaice can grow to a length of 50 cm (20"). They are best served poached, fried or grilled but care has to be taken not to overcook as the flesh is extremely tender. This fish goes very well with cranberry sauce.

Sole:
This is a dextral flat fish, which means they have their eyes on the right hand side. Sole can grow to a maximum length of 50 cm (20"). When serving, grilled sole should only be served with lemon butter. Filleted sole can be pan fried and served with either tartar sauce or Normandy sauce both of which complement the fish well. There is no fish called lemon sole and the only sole there is takes its name from Dover which is where the fish 'Dover sole' originates from.

Halibut:

Halibut, which grows to a length of about 2.5 m (8') and weighs as much as 300 kg (650 lb), is the largest of all flat fish. It comes from the cold waters of the North Atlantic and can be found from the Artic down to New Jersey and even Scotland. The name Halibut used to be spelled "Holibut " meaning "Holy" but the origins of its name are not clear. The flesh of halibut is coarse and dry and the fish needs to have a sauce as an accompaniment.

Dog fish:

Are a smaller species of shark, having tough, rough, sand papery skins which grow to a maximum length of 60–120 cm (24"- 48"). In some countries dog fish have been given more flattering names. For instance, in England it is known as "rock salmon" and in Italy "Vitello di Mare" which translates as " the veal of the sea." Dog fish is similar to Shark in that its flesh has no delicate flavour and its body is cartilaginous. It is good when served as fish and chips and also goes very well with sauces.

Angel shark:

This fish which has unusual features and many interesting names is correctly termed a shark. With shoulders resembling the cloak of a monk and a man's face in appearance, angel shark has been referred to as monk fish, Bishop and even Archbishop fish. Although angel shark doesn't resemble a conventional shark in looks, it is none-the-less cartilaginous and grows to a length of approximately 1.5 m (5'). It is a perfect fish for baking.

Skate:

This fish is also known as Ray and, like shark, has no true bones but is cartilaginous. Skate lives at the bottom of the sea and possesses a back colouring with which it is able to camouflage itself. Skate is best eaten after a couple of days and served with herbed butter.

Lobster:

This shellfish can live to a great age and grow to an extraordinary size of up to 1 m (3'3"). The heaviest recorded was caught in 1930 and weighed 20kg (45 lb). Nowadays lobsters half this size are considered giants. A lobster's natural colour is dark blue or green but once cooked, the shell turns bright red like a cardinals hat. Lobster goes very well with Thermidor, Newburg or à l'Américaine sauce.

Shrimps:
The name shrimp is the term associated with smaller species in the food industry, whereas prawns are the more special of the two names and the larger form. In North America the term "prawn" is practically obsolete and has almost entirely been replaced by the word shrimp. If prawn is used in America, it refers to the smaller species. (From: English Oxford Dictionary and American Webster's Dictionary). Shrimps whilst alive have a translucent appearance but when briefly boiled they become opaque. The flesh can either be eaten or turned into paste because of its strong flavour.

Prawns:
The maximum length of recorded prawns has been 22 cm (9"). The colour of prawns can vary from pale brown to greenish to pink and red. The prawns from Indo Pacific can reach lengths of up to 33 cm (13") and are known as tiger prawns.

Crab:
The most common crabs are the ones from northern Europe which are found in the waters of the western Mediterranean. Crabs can grow to a maximum width of 25 cm (10") and weigh as much as 5 kg (11 lbs.) The white meat in crabs comes only from its claws and the brown meat from its body. Crabs should feel heavy, and if shaken there should be no sound of liquid swilling around inside. The claws should also not hang down but should be tucked up against the body.

Cuttlefish:
The name cuttlefish means "head footed" and refers to the way in which the arms and tentacles sprout from their heads. Like octopus and squid, cuttlefish possess ink sacs and use the ink to screen their bodies and escape from predators. Although, the average length of the body is 25 cm (10") it can grow to a maximum length of 50 cm (20") long. Cuttlefish and squid are both known as the ink fish. In China they are called "the clerk of the god of the sea" and in Hong Kong they are known as the "black chief". Cuttlefish can be cooked in exactly the same way as squid.

Octopus:
This fish is known as Devil fish in America and Pearls of the Sea to divers. The flesh of octopus should be tenderised before cooking. Octopus has a more commercial importance than squid or cuttlefish. The usual market length of octopus is 50cm-1m (20"-40") but it can grow to three times this length. In Hong Kong larger species are called "laai por" meaning "muddy old woman" and smaller ones "saa lui" meaning sand bird.

Squid:
This fish occurs in all oceans and seas except the black sea. By 1980 one million tons were caught. The Japanese and Mediterranean people are more advanced in preparing and cooking this fish. With eight arms, swimming fins at the rear and a head with two long tentacles, squid swim near the surface of the water and are transparent in appearance. Some squid are known as flying squid and although they don't actually fly, they propel themselves momentarily out of the water before gliding back in. Squids have a single bone which can be removed easily and can be cooked, stuffed, ringed and deep fried as part of the Italian tradition "Frittura Mista", or on its own as Calamari and served with lemon wedges.

Oysters:
Oysters, the most prized and cultivated of shellfish, have the reputation of being "the pearl of the sea" and are considered a luxury food throughout the world. Oysters, should be eaten straight from the shell.

Scallops:
Alive, this shellfish is totally different from the one you buy at the fish market. Scallops do not crawl or burrow but move by opening and closing their shells. There are a great many different varieties of scallops in the world but the best known ones are the large "queen scallops" which have a maximum size of 10 cm. (4"). The colour of the shells of scallops can vary from yellow to pink, to purple or brown. One of the most esteemed ways to cook scallops is in cider or Muscadet.

Mussels:

These shellfish grow in clusters attached to rocks or other supports such as gravel beaches. Mussels have a greenish black shell which turns yellow after being exposed to the sun. Mussels are generally 10 cm (4") long but can grow to twice this length. They are cultured, plump and delicious to eat. The best known mussels come from Wimereux near Boulogne in France and have an excellent flavour and possess clean, pretty shells. Mussels have a reputation of being "unpaid monitors of water pollution" as they can accumulate toxins. In Belgium the national dish is " Moules et Frites". Italians use mussels for "zuppa di cozze," the French for "Moules Marinière" and the Spanish in " Paella".

Cockles:

The maximum length of cockles is about 6 cm (2") and the colour of the shell is brown, pale yellow or grubby white. In Britain cockles abound in sandy shores. Cockles are known by many names including ark shells, dog cockles and bloody cockles. They can be eaten raw or in sauces with pasta.

Clams:

Clams gape, which is why they tend to be sandy and gritty. The surf clam, bar clam, hen clam, or sea clam are larger and have hard shells and are best eaten raw. In a bushel you could expect the following: little necks (450-650), cherry stones (300-325), medium stones (180) and chowders (125). The larger specimens are called sharps. Clams are best battered and fried.

Equipment

Only you can know what you need, but here I give a few guidelines as to the equipment that I find I use most often:

Food processor with mixer and blender.

Knives and good sharp ones. You should have a carbon steel 7 inch (18 cm) flexible filleting knife, a 5 inch (13 cm) cook's knife for general use, and a large 8 inch (20 cm) chopping knife with broad blade useful for chopping herbs, mushrooms and onions.

Chopping boards - wooden ones are definitely better, a small 6 inch (15 cm) for cutting lemon wedges and garlic, and one at least 18 inches (45 cm) square.

Spatula - long stainless steel fish slice.

Slotted spoon - stainless steel for lifting the fish from stock and testing vegetables when boiling, etc.

Scissors - the kitchen type to cut the fins off fish and for gutting.

Sieve or strainer, stainless steel is best

Grater - 4 sided small toothed hand grater.

Pastry brush - for brushing the fish with melted butter or oil while grilling.

Saucepans - large and small.

Frying pans - a 12 inch pan with lid and a deep fat frying pan with wire basket.

Baking tray - for putting your salmon or sea bass in after wrapping them with aluminium foil.

Whisks - 2 kinds, a wheel whisk and a wire whisk.

Terminology

Aspic: cold food glazed with jelly

Baste: moisten the food by pouring hot liquid or oil over it.

Bisque: thick creamy sea food soup.

Bouquet garni: is made up of bay leaf, parsley and thyme wrapped up in muslin.

Braise: to brown ingredients in a little oil or fat at a high temperature.

Cayenne: chilli powder, hot red pepper.

Court-Bouillon: to poach fish in water, wine and herbs.

Cream: to soften and blend ingredients to a consistency of cream.

Curdle: when ingredients separate with lumpy result.

Dredge: to cover completely with flour or bread crumbs.
Fumet: a reduced fish stock.
Glaze: to brush with a beaten egg before baking to give shine to pastry.
Infuse: extract flavour from food by steeping in hot liquid.
Marinade: is to steep food in vinegar, lemon juice, oil and wine which is highly seasoned to make it more tender.
Paprika: sweet red pepper.
Parcook: to pre cook or cook partially.
Pepper: black pepper, white pepper.
Pimento: sweet peppers, bell peppers, capsicum.
Poach: to cook gently in a simmering liquid.
Pound: to tenderise with a mallet.
Purée: to press through a fine sieve.
Roux: butter and flour cooked over a low heat.
Sauté: to fry and brown evenly in a little oil or butter.
Score: to make evenly spaced cuts to allow flavouring to penetrate into the fish.
Sear: to brown the surface of fish quickly over high heat.
Souse: to pickle oily fish in vinegar or brine.

Herbs & spices

Fresh herbs have a more refined flavour than dried or frozen ones. Herbs lend themselves to creative cooking. Try to use what fresh herbs you need and freeze the rest immediately. The herbs and seasoning I enjoy using when I intend to flavour a fish are as follows:

Basil, bay leaves, cinnamon, cumin, cloves, chilli powder, dill, fennel, chervil, garlic, ginger, marjoram, mustard seeds, nutmeg, oregano, parsley, pepper cracked and black, paprika, rosemary, saffron, tarragon, thyme, turmeric.

Imperial– Metric Conversion

I have tried to make these conversions as accurate as possible. My personal view is to use these only as a sort of guideline and not to let the mathematical equations dampen your good spirit.

1oz	30g	10oz	280g	1 ¾ lb	785g
2	55	11	310	2	900
3	85	12	335	2 ½	1.1kg
4	110	13	365	3	1.35
5	140	14	390	3 ½	1.55
6	170	15	420	4	1.8
7	195	1 lb	450	4 ½	2
8	225	1 ¼ lb	550	5	2.25
9	250	1 ½ lb	670		

Weights: 1 oz = 28g   1000g = 1 kg   1 kg = 2.2 lb or 2 lb 3 oz

Volumes: 1 pint = 20 fl oz   ¼ pint = 5 fl oz = 150 ml

½ pint	300 ml
¾	425
1	550
1¼	600
1½	850
1¾	1 litre
2 pints (1 quart)	1.1 litre

Lengths: These measurments are approximate conversions from Metric to Imperial but, Metrication is the order of the day.

5 mm	¼ inch
10 mm = 1 cm	½ inch
2 cm	¾ inch
2.5 cm	1 inch
30.5 cm	12 inches = 1 foot
91.5 cm	36 inches = 1 yard
100 cm = 1 meter	39 inches

Oven Temperatures

Only you know how accurate your oven is and the type of oven you are using.

In conventional ovens, the temperature is hottest at the top whereas, in convection ovens the temperature is hotter where the fan is. Please allow at least 15 minutes to pre-heat your oven and use stated cooking times only as guidelines.

Gas Mark	Fahrenheit	Celsius	Description
¼	225°	110°	Very cold
½	250	130	
1	275	140	Cool
2	300	150	
3	325	170	Warm
4	350	180	Moderate
5	375	190	Moderately hot
6	400	200	
7	425	220	Hot
8	450	230	
9	475	240	Very hot

Index

T

V

By the same author:

Elaborate Cooking Uncovered

From classic to modern contemporary dishes and from Traditional to Nouvelle cuisine for everyone, with many dishes and recipes from around the world

Obtainable through:

www.elaboratecookinguncovered.com

Or major stockists or

Le Chateau Ali
Nottingham

Notes

Notes

Notes

Notes

Notes